Grounded

Grounded

The off-road guide to parenting in an unstable world

DR MICHAEL C. NAGEL
and **DR SHELLEY DAVIDOW**

© Michael C. Nagel and Shelley Davidow 2024

All rights reserved. No part of this book may be reproduced or transmitted in any form or by any means, electronic or mechanical, including photocopying, recording or by any information storage and retrieval system, without prior permission in writing from the publisher.

Published by Amba Press
Melbourne, Australia
www.ambapress.com.au

Editor: Andrew Campbell
Cover designer: Tess McCabe

Printed by IngramSpark

ISBN: 9781923116290 (pbk)
ISBN: 9781923116306 (ebk)

A catalogue record for this book is available from the National Library of Australia.

Dedicated to all the parents who give unselfishly to ensure they do right by their children

Contents

Acknowledgements	ix
Introduction	1
1 Understanding the Brain	9
2 Buffering Young Hearts and Minds	25
3 This Is Your Brain on Adolescence!	39
4 Focus on Resilience Instead of Trauma	53
5 Know Thy Child's School Well	67
6 Building Resilience in the Real World	79
7 Fear Not!	95
8 Taking Care of Yourself Is Not Selfish	111
9 Nurturing a Healthy and Happy Mind	129
10 Keep Calm and Carry On!	145
About the Authors	153
Endnotes	155
References	159
Index	165

Acknowledgements

Which is more difficult – writing a book or being a parent? From our standpoint we would suggest the latter. Books have a certain structure, plenty of opportunities to edit and correct, and there is always an ending. Parenting ebbs and flows. Sometimes parents are holding a steady course with wind in the sails, and other times they are navigating through storms of chaos. Editing and correcting for parents is called trial and error, with equal shares of success and failure. And to be sure, being a parent never really ends… yes, we know that there is an ultimate ending, but that is a bit too dark to consider here. What we are trying to say is that it ain't easy being a parent. We want to acknowledge that truism, and our hope in writing this book is that we might help support and guide parents along the way.

We'd like to acknowledge all those people – too many to list here – who have helped shape our ideas, experiences and souls as authors, researchers, educators and most importantly parents. We have been fortunate to have had our collective thoughts, insights and philosophies formed through the interactions of so many people across many countries. That collective permeates much of this book.

We would also like to acknowledge and thank Andrew Campbell, our editor, for pointing out any errors in our writing and taking our words and ensuring they flow smoothly. We have written many books and articles but there is always room for improvement and Andrew has provided that. And finally, our heartfelt thanks to Alicia Cohen of Amba Press not only for supporting our work and providing a vehicle to get our thoughts out to the world but also for her unwavering belief in our message.

Introduction

Childhood is a brief, potent, potentially exquisite time that we only get to experience once. This relatively small window of time in our lives shapes so much of who we become as adults. What wounds will we carry? What capacities will we have to not only survive but thrive and fulfil our dreams in the world?

Parenthood, on the other hand, can seem to last an eternity. In terms of raising offspring, no other child-rearing species on the planet requires the lengthy and loving commitment that an adult human must deliver over many years. And even when children grow into adulthood, they never really leave their parents. Sure, they might be some distance away geographically, but children are forever connected to their parents, and parents are forever parenting, or so it might seem. Bearing all this in mind, we thought it would be helpful for parents to engage with ideas related to parenting that have stood the test of time, research that reinforces those ideas, and an optimistic look at what the world has to offer our children. We also thought it important to spend some time focusing on how parents can take care of themselves.

We are authors. However, we are also parents, educators and academics. For this book, we draw on our collective decades of research, parenting and hard-won insights and bring all of that together with this purpose: to offer parents (of tots to teens) a guide to protecting childhood and supporting children's developing nervous systems while also taking care of their own. Fulfilling such a goal is not only good for the child but also good for the parent. The overall intent is to offer insights into how to minimise the effects of stress and support optimum cognitive, emotional and physiological development, at home, at school and out in the world. The guide is informed by neuroscientific, psychological and educational research and our own lived experiences as parents.

It is important for you to remember that we are parents, and we think that gives us a degree of "street cred" to go along with our professional personas. Drawing on all of this, we believe that if we want children to enjoy childhood and become happy, healthy adults in a world that can seem increasingly frightening to many, there is much we can do. No, we are not suggesting filling the lives of children with extracurricular activities to somehow build a vast array of capacities that might normally unfold if allowed to do so on their own. Instead, we contend that much of what we need to do is well understood in the research literature and through the experiences of past generations of parents. This is what we want to share with you. And as the title of the book states, this journey requires going "off-road" - getting off the "stress freeway" and doing the simple things. These things often fall by the roadside because parents believe they are time poor or that they must invest their energies into building their child's academic résumés before they celebrate their fifth birthday. Things like just playing, being in nature, baking, making things, or allowing kids to simply be bored are forgotten or shunned in lieu of building the perfect child.

In order to support our beliefs, and hopefully influence yours, we lay out the developmental essentials that allow children to experience a grounded childhood that sets them up to be resilient, balanced, empathetic adults. As parents, we can do a lot to mitigate stress in their lives - but we also need to learn to allow them to fall and get back up again on their own. We can respond to our children's challenges, issues and behaviours in ways that help them to not only survive but thrive, without having to designate "safe" spaces for them at every turn.

Now, we also would readily agree that the world we knew only a few short years ago has changed in some ways beyond recognition. We are troubled in the knowledge that as parents many of us are more anxious, concerned and protective of our children than previous generations of parents. The fallout of the last couple of years of global panic has impacted children significantly, raising their anxieties along with ours. In case you have forgotten, the world changed in a way we had never experienced in our lifetimes at the end of 2019. The events following the announcement of a coronavirus pandemic raised our anxiety and stress levels and – dare we say – traumatised us and our children.

Until that time, we – the authors – had never really used the word "trauma" as part of our regular vernacular. Sure, we knew of traumatic events and had heard of mental health issues such as post-traumatic stress disorder, but we had never really considered ourselves to be in a state of trauma. This in turn got us thinking about children and trauma. You see, as researchers, authors, educators, educators of future educators, and parents, we have an innate switch that, when flipped, shines a light of curiosity on anything to do with children. Once that light has been switched on, we often find ourselves asking questions about what we do to, and with, children and teens in our homes, in schools and out in the world.

The numerous disruptions to our lives during the pandemic have led us to believe, more strongly than ever, that it's time to let children just be children. It might also interest you to know that the pandemic only exacerbated a worrying trend over the last couple of decades. Before the turn of the century, and according to most available psychological measures, children growing up in the modern industrialised western world were calmer, better adjusted, less impacted by mental health issues, more resilient and, most importantly, happier than their predecessors! So what happened? This is something we tease out in the pages that follow by taking a critical look at not only ourselves and our home environments but also our schools and attitudes about life and the world around us. We do so with a view to ensuring that our kids are not being treated as pawns to be anxiously moved along political or ideological pathways based on someone else's preconceived notions of the world or their place in it. As educators, we think schools are especially significant environments to consider.

It is important to look at school environments because outside of the home this is where children spend most of their time. So much so that teachers are trained with some Latin in mind: *in loco parentis* is a phrase meaning "in the place of a parent" and it underpins the excellent work teachers do in schools. However, this transfer of parental responsibilities is limited and short-lived and should never exist without scrutiny. When children arrive at school every day, they are immersed in an environment that ideally should mirror aspects of the care, protection and behaviour of a home with a positive and responsible parent. This places a tremendous amount of moral and legal responsibility on teachers to create an environment of safety and security. Sometimes, however, well-meaning intentions in schools may actually be misplaced or misinformed, or may not mirror parental desires, resulting in unintended negative consequences. We will explore this in detail in the second section of this book.

As researchers, we also believe that anything we do to and with children should be based on the best available evidence, and with this in mind we offer insights into what constitutes healthy parental and educational practice for all children. The foundation for such insights are based on an optimistic outlook, supported by empirical evidence, suggesting that the world is actually in pretty good shape. Our children, and you, need to know that they, and you, will be okay. In spite of what you might see or hear via the news, the world is not a place of danger and despair. The opportunities for children today exceed those of any previous generation, and the information in this book will offer parents a foundation for considering what is really important for children to develop into healthily functioning teens and adults.

At its core, we offer this book as a parenting companion. Use what's useful. Take it as a jump-off point. We don't suggest that anyone should outsource their own wisdom and parenting intuition, nor their critical thinking. This sentiment permeates our writing and underpins our philosophies of life and learning and our belief that travelling off-road is often the best place to be. In order to get that journey started, here is what you can expect to explore in the following pages.

The first section of the book focuses on the home environment. We start by looking at key factors in healthy child development and unpack how the brain develops in utero and matures from birth. The focus here is on how this development can be fostered proactively and positively. We make reference to various aspects of development, but our primary focus is on cognitive and socio-emotional development. We draw on decades of research in various branches of psychology coupled with contemporary insights from neuroscientific research to offer the reader key thoughts on the most important ingredients for ensuring healthy development.

With a foundation of understanding brain development in mind (pun intended), Chapter 2 then takes what we know about healthy development and describes what can hinder that process. The focus here is on the hearts and minds of young children. Specifically, we examine three significant mechanisms that can have a negative impact on overall development, namely anxiety, stress and trauma. We also look at these variables in the context of how you, the parent, can stay stress-free. Anxiety, stress and trauma may be interrelated in some ways, but each has a number of specific variables that are worthy of discussion when it comes to childhood and parenthood.

In the third and final chapter of this section of the book, we explore what is healthy for "tweens" and "teens". Perhaps no other time in parenthood can be as challenging as that of the teenage years. Consequently, we look at how developmental changes through adolescence can be supported best by parents and how parents can further enhance the home environment when hormones take over the bodies and minds of their children.

The second section of the book shifts the focus away from the home and into the wider environment. Chapter 4 begins by extending previous discussions and examining the pernicious nature of trauma.

We aim to extend the reader's understanding of trauma by looking at some case studies to provide insights into the diverse nature of events that could be described as actually traumatic. We then look at the prevalence of trauma among current populations of children and what happens with traumatised children in school. We also note how "schooling", the media and government bureaucracies might actually be contributing to anxiety, stress and trauma in children and teens. We wrap this chapter up by outlining the important role parents play in taking care of themselves and modelling how to face anxiety and stress.

Chapter 5 moves beyond the challenges noted in the previous chapter and further examines what educators can do to ensure that children thrive in their respective schooling environments. This examination is punctuated by poking holes in a number of well-intentioned educational initiatives. Current educational endeavour is rife with good intentions and seemingly commonsensical policies that we contend are, in fact, doing more harm than good. We think parents should know about this and be informed consumers of worthy educational practices founded in actual research rather than the whimsical notions of learning and teaching often found in glossy government reports.

After school, it's time to look at the world. The third section of our book starts by exploring the myths and realities associated with growing up in our current social and cultural milieu. It is our contention that the 24/7 news cycle and the omnipresence of technology and social media have fostered stress, fear and anxiety for those yet to move into adulthood. We concede that there are challenges and safety concerns for raising healthy and happy young people, but fears around child safety, abduction, the plight of the planet and other "world fears" need to be tempered with the reality that on most measures the world is actually a better, safer place than the one often presented to children. Within this mindset, we explore how parents and teachers can build resilience and positivity in young people while also making the mind the best "safe space" available to all.

Chapter 7 then presents a cautionary tale of how society has travelled down a road of pathologising life and childhood, with fear permeating much of the cultural and social zeitgeist. We also posit that so much of what was simply seen as aspects of diversity among young people in previous generations has been enveloped within agendas that seek to diagnose (with the aim of "protecting") current generations and young minds. This chapter is not about attributing any measure of blame to anyone or anything in particular but instead looks to nurture what has become known as a "growth mindset".

The final section of the book is about being grounded and taking into account where you are in the moment. Chapter 8 opens this discussion by focusing on parents caring for themselves and ensuring their respective roles are not hijacked by anxiety or stress. We offer key strategies to enable adults, educators and parents alike to achieve a calm mind. It is our contention that this is the bedrock for ensuring that the same mind can support young people in the most positive way possible – which segues nicely into Chapter 9.

Chapter 9 is all about the "kids"! Within a framework of care and compassion, this chapter extends earlier insights into helping children deal with anxiety, stress and trauma. We focus on the importance of relationships and offer strategies on how adults can help children to calm their hearts and minds by supporting their nervous system. In order to help facilitate calmness, the chapter also offers evidence of the importance of the arts, nature and playfulness. We present insights into how those areas can act as a buffer against the competitive nature of "schooling" and as a better array of tools for helping children who are struggling. Sometimes the most potent things we can do to protect children are also the most common-sense approaches.

The final chapter of the book returns to you. It pulls all the key points from the previous chapters into a framework for working on the best version of you. We review the main points of the book and provide final thoughts on creating home and learning environments that "ground" children in the present, assist them to become themselves without fear and anxiety, and encourage parents, caregivers and teachers to go "off-road" and find the pathways that work to support optimal development. We aim to remind adults who care for and work with children that there is a toolkit for nurturing healthy hearts and minds, and that toolkit begins with you.

Understanding the Brain

"... we represent the highest expression of a trick that Mother Nature discovered: don't entirely pre-script the brain; instead, just set it up with the basic building blocks and get it into the world."

– Dr David Eagleman[1]

A Bit About the Brain and Early Development

One cubic millimetre! The size of a grain of sand! That minuscule fragment of human cortex, or brain matter, could hold about 2 petabytes of data. Neuroscientists have estimated that the entire human brain holds about 200 exabytes of information. Believe us, those are large numbers. Two petabytes would be enough to store all the movies ever made, including their trailers, and 200 exabytes is roughly equal to the entire digital content of the world. In other words, your brain could store all the data available on the internet along with all the data on every digital storage device on the planet. This information was published in one of the world's most prestigious neuroscientific journals and made news headlines globally, creating fodder for writers and brain enthusiasts alike.[2] For us, it is a reminder of the unimaginable power of the gelatinous mass between our ears.

Strangely enough, and barring any injuries or health problems, we don't often think about our brains. We tend to take them for granted and don't realise that the brain is responsible for regulating every breath, step and heartbeat in our lifetime. It takes in millions of bits of information every second so we can hear, taste, touch, smell and see all that we desire. The brain is our centre for survival and our hub for learning how to speak, sensing another's pain, falling in love, making good and bad decisions, and reading the words on this page. As neuroscientist Joseph LeDoux has so eloquently noted, it is the most unimaginable thing imaginable.

An understanding of the brain is critical to our discussions throughout this book. For example, if you are going to have a better understanding of the pernicious effects of stress and anxiety and how to manage them effectively for you and your children, then some basic neuroscience is in order. We need to start this exploration from the beginning, or more specifically from roughly 17 days after conception.

Many women may not even be aware that they are pregnant when the foundations for a child's brain are being laid. Not long after conception, neurons, the building blocks of our interconnected neural superhighway, begin to emerge. Neurons are nerve cells that act as information messengers, and while the brain does not actually begin to look like itself until roughly five to seven weeks into gestation, neurons are busy building the initial nervous system earlier. This rapid proliferation of neurons continues in utero and then explodes into a big bang of synaptic activity at birth.

You likely have heard of the term "synapses" and have some sense of what that word means. If not, then here is a simple overview. Synapses are electro-chemical signals that travel from one neuron to another. These signals occur as our brain interprets stimulation from the environment via our senses. The more repetitive the stimulation, the greater the potential for creating long-term connections between neurons. Neuroscientists have many catchy sayings to explain the brain's activity, and here's one for you: *As neurons fire together, they wire together!* Amazingly, no two neurons in your brain physically touch. We use the word "amazingly" because the 100 billion or so neurons you have in your head are supporting more pathways than there are stars and planets in our solar system. It is estimated that the possible number of connections between our neurons is so large we don't even have a number to describe it ... think one followed by a million zeros.

An important thing to remember here is the fact that neurons convey information through an electro-chemical impulse. We will talk more about how this happens later, but at this stage here is something to consider – the introduction of other chemicals in utero, as taken in by the mother, can impact on those transmissions. It is wise, therefore, to consider lifestyle choices such as drinking, smoking, drug use or exposure to environmental toxins when trying to become pregnant, rather than waiting for a positive pregnancy test; by the time a mother finds out she is pregnant, neurons may already be actively communicating to one another while being hindered by foreign toxins such as alcohol, nicotine and some medications. So, when moving through the nine months of pregnancy, it is imperative to ensure, as best as possible, that the womb is a healthy environment. A healthy mother, and by association womb, helps to lay the groundwork for all aspects of healthy development of the child.

One final thought before looking at how the brain develops after birth is the potential impact of maternal stress on a child's brain in utero. Later in the book we give specific details about the physiological impact of stress and the chemical firestorm that stress can cause to the body and brain. Suffice it to say, for now, that an expectant mother who is stressed or anxious may be creating future challenges for her offspring. In fact, it turns out that stress-related problems can even span across more than one generation. If Mum's expected child is female, then that unborn child is already producing ova. The science of epigenetics tells us that Mum's stress may not only impact on her daughter but also on the eggs her daughter is growing, leaving future generations susceptible to negative outcomes resulting from whatever Grandma was going through while pregnant.

Okay, let's get back to brain development with a quick refresher: neurons are the building blocks of the brain that start their amazing work early in pregnancy by sending information to one another via synapses. In one sense the passing of information from one neuron to the other is the purest form of "learning", given that neurons build connections via stimulation from the outside world and these connections can become permanent pathways, depending on the duration and repetition of stimulation. The brain is very efficient as well, for it actually operates on a "use it or lose it" principle (another clever neuroscientific catch-phrase); only those connections and pathways that are activated frequently are retained. Other connections that are not consistently used will be pruned or discarded so the active connections can become stronger. This is a natural phenomenon and is even more pronounced during adolescence when the brain is restructuring itself. We will take a long look at the teenage brain in Chapter 3. For now, let's unpack what happens after being born!

The Developing Brain After Birth

On the eventful day a child is born, its brain's basic building blocks are now exposed to an exponential growth of stimulation. Sights and sounds coupled with smells, tastes and human touch bombard the infant brain with so much information that by the time that child reaches its third birthday it will have more neural connections than its paediatrician. An infant's brain actually has more neurons than it will eventually need and overcompensates in synaptic production as a way of hedging its bets towards healthy neural functioning. Remember, Mother Nature doesn't entirely pre-script the brain but instead allows it to soak up information and design itself through experience.

The first three to four years of life are very significant for the developing brain. This is a time when the brain is very active, making sense of the world and building life-long connections;

a time when oral language begins to emerge, and all other aspects of development have their groundwork laid. This is also a time when the brain actually *expects* some types of experiences to occur and *depends* on others on the road to normal development. For example, in order for a child's visual system to develop properly, the brain expects to have opportunities to see things, and visual stimulation obviously becomes much more readily available after birth. Every time an infant sees something, hears something, smells something, tastes something or feels something, its brain is rapidly building a network of neural complexity.

In contrast to the experiences a child's brain expects, the experiences it depends on are those that arise from opportunities within specific contexts and the unique features of a child's individual environment. You might consider these the moments that are provided to a child by the people or things around it. So, while a child *expects* to hear language in order to learn to speak, the language it learns will *depend* on what is being spoken within its environment; being born in Spain means the brain will learn to speak and think in Spanish.

In a way, what the brain expects and depends on could be labelled as nature and nurture respectively, and both play a part in helping shape the developing brain. Nature lays the groundwork for a functioning mind, and we nurture that mind through the experiences we actively provide. Remember too that whatever the experiences, connections become stronger and more efficient through repeated use. Reading to children every day, for example, helps strengthen essential connections for later literacy development. Some very important connections are made stronger when children have daily opportunities to develop both large and small muscle skills, have the chance to practise developing social skills, and interact directly with their environment. This is one of the reasons why "play" is such a critical component of activity across all aspects of development. Playful endeavour is a cornerstone of healthy development, and when we say "play" we are not talking about doing so in a virtual world. Children need to play with other children and adults in real time and in real places. The literature on child development is quite clear: the absence of play leads to measurable declines in all areas of development.

It is also vital to incorporate rich language into all activities, since exposure to rich language creates the foundation for a child's use and understanding of words and increases the likelihood of reading success at a later age. When we speak of rich language, we are talking about increasingly exposing children to greater complexity of words and sentences. This starts when adults speak "parentese".

You may not have heard of parentese before, but it is that "singsongy" type of speaking that adults will use when talking to infants. Some people might call it baby talk. It sounds a bit like singing, with its elongated vowels, repetitions and over-pronounced syllables. Interestingly, parentese happens in all cultures and across all languages, leading neuroscientists to believe it is innate and plays a special role in the initial stages of oral language development. Parentese is an important component of early communication, but over time a child needs to hear lots of different words, phrases and sentences in increasingly complex oral structures. Parentese gives way to the development of typical speech patterns between people, and the greater the number of words used and modelled with a child, the better.

We know that the richness of a young child's verbal interactions has a dramatic effect on vocabulary and school readiness, and that differences are correlated with socio-economic status. A watershed study conducted by researchers in the United States found that, by age 3, the observed cumulative vocabulary for children in professional families was 1,116 words; for working class families it was about 740; and for welfare families 525. The most significant differences between those demographics were the number of verbal interactions that occurred each day between adults and children and the richness of language used.[3] In other words, interacting with children through a mosaic of vocabulary is the best precursor to developing oral language and by association scholastic success.

And once again, play becomes integral to the types of interactions needed for a developing brain.

What Not to Do With the Developing Brain

To reiterate, providing playful opportunities enriched with conversation helps the developing brain. Playing and talking also reinforce the notion that human beings are, by their very nature, social beings. Those two simple activities also tell us that parents do not have to schedule extra tuition for their children or build an academic résumé before a child's fifth birthday. In fact, trying to do too much too soon or build a better brain may do more harm than good. While stimulation from the environment is important, it is misleading to think that a child's brain can be improved or that learning can be accelerated by providing excessive levels of stimulation. The last couple of decades have seen an expanding market of brain-"enriching" toys and/or tuition programs purporting to do everything from teaching two-year-olds to read to making bilingual babies via language DVDs. And more recently the pervasive push to have children on screen devices for learning is bearing some pretty rotten fruit.

At this juncture there are some things to always keep in mind. The brain actually has a neurological timetable that extends from birth through childhood and into adulthood, which is mediated by various developmental processes and is potentially hindered by mistimed interventions or contrived learning endeavours. To put this into context and at the risk of being too technical, it is important to know about something in our heads called "myelin".

While you may never have heard of myelin, you may be familiar with the fact that the brain has both grey and white matter. The white matter is myelin, which is actually a type of fat that insulates the axons of neurons. Axons are like little wires that help in passing information from one end of a neuron (nucleus and dendrites) to the other end (axon terminals) and then on to other neurons' dendrites.

At birth we have far less myelin (white matter) than grey matter, and over the course of many years our brain will work to produce the requisite amount of myelin needed somewhere in our third decade of life. We are in effect working to become fatheads!

So why is myelin so significant? As noted earlier, myelin has insulating and protective qualities that aid in the transmission of information from one neuron to another, and the more "myelinated" axons we have in our brain, the greater the opportunity for neural information to be passed quickly. The end result of all of this is that certain activities may be easier to learn when regions of the brain are sufficiently myelinated or when our brains become "fatter".

The growth of myelin, or "myelination", is very important for children because newborn babies have very few myelinated axons. This is one reason why vision and motor coordination, for example, are so limited at birth; the neural networks responsible for facilitating vision and movement aren't working fast enough and will become much more efficient when myelin increases in conjunction with the experience of processing visual stimulation. Furthermore, as we grow older, different regions of the brain myelinate at different ages. For example, when Broca's area – the region of the brain responsible for language production – myelinates, children are then able to develop speech and grammar after hearing words and conversations. To that end, it is important to remember that a healthy brain knows which areas need to be myelinated first, that myelination cannot happen all at once, and that it cannot be accelerated via flashcards, extra tuition or the latest "learning" app on a tablet or phone.

That last point cannot be emphasised enough and is very important in terms of being "grounded" in your approach to raising your child. Over the last few decades, research has shown that trying to get children to do things too soon can actually result in a variety of anxiety-related disorders associated with stress. Doing more may actually result in achieving less! And sadly, neuroscience has often been misused by opportunists looking to make a buck by peddling brain-"enrichment" toys, early "learning" devices, and/or programs advocating increased education. Their modus operandi and business plan is to convince parents that the younger you "educate" a mind, the better. There is little, if any, evidence to support these notions or the idea that early and extra stimulation or enrichment activities lead to some measure of advanced brain development, improved intelligence or academic prowess. Always remember that unless children live in situations of extreme poverty, violence, isolation or social and emotional deprivation, the natural everyday environments they find themselves in will promote strong neural development and a healthy start to learning. Therefore, and in spite of what any infomercial citing "brain science" says about learning, the brain of a two-year-old, for example, is simply not ready, nor has it been scripted, to read or do many other things beyond its developmental timelines. However, there are some things that can be done at certain times that can help you to help your child.

"Actual" Opportunities for the Developing Brain

As we have seen, notions of enriching children's learning have led to the emergence of a vast empire of learning tools and apps in stores and online. Ideas surrounding enrichment have also encompassed a number of myths about how to improve the minds of children. For the record, the following claims are NOT true by any stretch of the imagination:

- Parents can boost cognitive development via "brain-friendly" toys and early enrichment programs.
- Exposing infants and toddlers to language DVDs will boost vocabulary.
- Playing Mozart to a child in utero will improve their math scores, and listening to classical music will make kids smarter.
- Through "proper" training with a "qualified" practitioner, the fundamental functions of the left and right hemispheres can be enhanced.

If you happen to see any such "mythinformation" online or in a bookstore, save your time and money by ignoring it. To date, there isn't any way to hyper-stimulate neural development or make children smarter. However, there are some things that, if willingly engaged with by the child, can reap positive outcomes. These things are once again founded on aspects of neural development and the growth of myelin.

As discussed earlier, at times when regions of the brain are myelinating, they are more responsive to certain stimulation. These time periods have been labelled by researchers as "learning windows" and represent the best times to engage in certain activities. Research around this concept mirrors that of sensitive periods noted earlier in relation to experience-expectant stimulation. However, unlike the critical period when an infant needs to see things to hardwire for sight, learning windows simply offer an optimum time for some activities, and these windows never completely close.

Before we delve further into positive aspects of learning windows, please ensure you stay grounded in the knowledge that these are not "must-dos" requiring you to search online for extra learning opportunities. Moreover, any engagement in the types of activities discussed below are best kept for when a child actively wants to engage in such activities. It is equally important that these activities be done with other people. The pixelated screens of a virtual world are no match for the richness of experiences between people, especially those of a child with other children and adults.

One example of a learning window can be found in the fact that the best time to learn a second or third language is between birth and roughly 11 years of age. This is a time when the brain is very receptive to all aspects of language development, native language and otherwise. This is not to say that a teenager or adult can never learn to speak Italian if they choose to do so – it will just involve more work and be a bit harder. It is also interesting to note that an abundance of research tells us that learning a second language not only seems to enrich a child's native language and future literacy in school, but also enhances various cognitive capacities and provides therapeutic benefits as they grow older. Researchers have discovered that learning a second language enhances concentration and attention, promotes earlier development of "theory of mind", and can delay the onset of dementia and other age-related cognitive deficits.[4]

A second example of an open learning window focuses on learning to play an instrument. Three to 11 years of age appears to be the best time to start strumming the strings of a guitar, learning to tickle the ivories of a piano, or playing any other type of instrument. Learning to play an instrument promotes many aspects of cognitive and physical development. There are studies that have shown that learning to play a musical instrument engages most regions of the brain and enhances neural connections between the left and right hemispheres, resulting in positive effects on learning, memory, reading ability, fine motor skills, verbal and non-verbal reasoning, and other executive functions. Some studies suggest that learning to play an instrument as a child may even be associated with better measures of academic performance and intelligence in adulthood.[5]

Once again, some caution is warranted for those who are now eagerly planning to get their children involved in learning a new language or musical instrument. A parent's desire to have their child engage in these types of activities must be balanced with the child's willingness to do so. The evidence tells us that children who learn another language or to play an instrument can reap some benefits, but we cannot emphasise enough that forcing them to do so or trying to do too much too soon is not "grounded" in any theory or practice. And while some might think that if experiences are indeed significant factors in neural development, then surely the earlier the stimulation (read "enrichment"), the greater the propensity for learning and early success. Yes, input from the environment does help shape the brain, and as noted experiences are important, but equally important is the fact that each child is an individual with similar but not identical developmental timelines – timelines that are more marathon than sprint in nature. This is even more pertinent than you might think, given the chasm between your child's emotional and rational brain.

Emotionally Charged and Cognitively Delayed

Earlier in the chapter we outlined some key elements of healthy brain development and the role of experiences in that development. To better understand how that can play out in the day-to-day realities of being a parent, it is also important to know a little about the regions of the brain and how they develop and impact behaviour over time.

When people hear the word "brain", they tend to picture the hemispheres of the brain. These two sections of the brain separate us from all other species on this planet. There are four lobes within these gelatinous structures, and each has its own array of regions that make us human. Our frontal, parietal, occipital and temporal lobes collectively forge our consciousness, allow us to think, provide a framework for comprehension and speech, and basically are responsible for most of the functions that make us human. And while there will not be a neuroanatomy quiz at the end of the chapter, it is important for you to comprehend the significance and magnificence of our frontal lobes.

The frontal lobes, as implied, sit at the front of the brain and are often referred to as the brain's chief executive officer or CEO. This is particularly true of the right prefrontal lobe, which sits just behind your right eye and is the last region of the brain to fully mature, somewhere in the mid-twenties. For both males and females, much of our brain is mature by our 18th or 19th birthday, with full maturation happening around 24 years of age for females and a bit later for males. While neuroscientists suggest that full maturation of the male brain does not occur until around 26 or so, for some of you the jury might still be out as to when this happens. That is the topic for another book but still worth noting with a bit of a chuckle.

You may be wondering why the frontal lobes are so important, and the simple answer is: this is where higher-order thinking processes and the regulation of emotions occur. When you make decisions, think about options, consider another person's feelings or put yourself in their place, or analyse situations and problems, it is the frontal lobes that are in action. They do a myriad of other things, but we think you get the point: damage your frontal lobes and your capacity to engage fully with the world will diminish markedly. They don't fully mature until later in life, as noted previously, which means children are often driven by their emotions. This is also true of teens, given that their brains go through a major restructuring once puberty starts to work its magic. But for now, let's focus on children!

Children are a great example of the brain's prime directives: to survive and learn – and in that order. At the base of the brain sits the brain stem, and nestled above it and surrounded by the hemispheres is the limbic system. The brain stem is the region of the brain that encourages you to fight or flee when threatened, and the limbic system is the emotional heart of the brain. Looking at its maturational trajectory, the brain matures from the bottom up and from the inside out. In other words, our survival mechanisms come online first, followed by our emotions and then finally our brain's higher-order CEO. You can observe this whenever a three-year-old troubles you for something to eat while you are making dinner. If you say no to a snack, you will likely encounter a sudden mood change resulting in the child curled up in a foetal position on the floor proclaiming they are starving. Their immature brain thinks that if they don't eat right then and there they are literally going to die. Survival, then learning, is the brain's way of moving forward, and a hungry three-year-old doesn't have the capacity to think through responsible options. Over time, and with guidance, that three-year-old will mature and learn that having a snack is not a matter of life or death and that its parent is not evil. Moreover – and not unlike the ins and outs of developmental timelines noted earlier – it is not possible to accelerate emotional maturation.

The limbic system has its own developmental clock, so adults must do what they can to avoid overwhelming a child's emotional world. Once again, it is important to acknowledge that trying to push children to do things too soon may ultimately engulf them in negative emotions and undue stress beyond their evolving coping abilities. The next chapter takes a deep dive into the impact of stress, anxiety and trauma on children, and so we finish with this final note.

For all children, the road to nurturing healthy brain development is not too difficult for parents, teachers and other caregivers to follow. Children do not have to be hyper-stimulated or prepped for university by the time they are five years old. What will help them, however, are regular routines and consistency, opportunities to consolidate learning through repetition, hands-on interactions and activities, novel ways to learn through exploration and experimentation, exposure to rich, interactive language, and most importantly, positive, reliable, supportive and stress-free relationships.

Ground Rules

1. The brain begins to develop early in utero, and it would be wise to avoid alcohol, environmental toxins and drugs when trying to fall pregnant. A healthy womb makes for positive development.

2. Stress in mums can lead to issues for the unborn child as well as future generations. Find ways to ameliorate or avoid stress if possible.

3. Brain development – and by association all other aspects of development – has innate timelines that are more marathon than sprint, so forget trying to hyper-stimulate learning or hyper-educate the young mind.

4. Fostering playful activities and paying attention to oral language are precursors for all aspects of development and future success at school.

5. Willing participation by a child in learning a second language or playing a musical instrument can lead to long-term benefits.

Two

Buffering Young Hearts and Minds

"It's a tough world out there, and the sooner my kid gets used to it, the better."

– Anonymous parent

Early Exposure to Stress

You've probably heard the opening quote before. Maybe you've even said it when your kids were confronted with something stressful or unpleasant. Many people may believe this "the sooner the better" scenario. The problem is, as it turns out – it isn't true. Exposing kids prematurely to stressful situations does not make them better at dealing with stress – in fact, exactly the opposite.

What happens early on is written into neural circuitry – so, as we saw in Chapter 1, any environment or experience that primes children for a fight-or-flight response is creating the blueprint for that child to have an overactive sympathetic nervous system. If a child is hit, or yelled at or exposed to real trauma before they can cognitively process or manage what is happening, they will have a heightened stress response to the world in general.

If we say we want to protect children and childhood, this does not mean we are attempting to make kids weak or incapable of confronting the world. Protecting children from undue stress while their brains are developing at a phenomenal rate will, in fact, set them up to have a measured, healthy response to the world when stress does come their way later on – which it will.

Have you ever wondered why some kids seem to just take the world in their stride – dealing with things both good and bad as if they're simply playing a game of table tennis? They hit a few balls, miss some, but nothing seems to put them on the wrong foot. And then there are those other kids who, faced with the exact same situations, fall to pieces. There are meltdowns and tantrums and tears, and these kids may experience small adversities as world-ending dramas.

As is turns out, the stress-response of your toddler may be the result of something that happened in utero, or even far back in the past – maybe even some generations ago. Remember the discussion of epigenetics in the previous chapter? Well, in his wonderful book *Why Zebras Don't Get Ulcers*, neuroscientist Robert Sapolsky provides a poignant example of epigenetics when he discusses how, when pregnant mothers are stressed, they are in fact "teaching" their babies in utero to have an overactive fight-or-flight response. "Anxiety revolves around a part of the brain called the amygdala, and prenatal stress programs the amygdala into a lifelong profile that has anxiety written all over it."[6]

Shelley tells this story:

> "I was such a pregnant mother. I was in South Africa and nine months pregnant. There were a few nightly break-ins on our property; in the country, the crime rate was so high that everyone knew someone who had been either hijacked, murdered, raped or assaulted. My fight-or-flight response was primed.
>
> I know I was way too stressed night and day, and flooding my body (and my baby's) with cortisol, adrenaline, and providing

the sound of my racing heart. My baby was already 'learning' about his immediate surroundings – my womb – and he was being conditioned to have an over-active stress-response.

There was the night we came back from a movie and 11 or 12 intruders were making their way through our property. They had robbed the house behind us, but I didn't know this. I thought they were in our house. I thought we were going to die that night. The amount of stress in my system could not have been more.

We survived this intrusion, but many South African families didn't and don't survive similar ones.

I was so terrified by the experience, that afterwards, any dog barking at night, any bump, crack or noise felt like something that heralded the end of our lives. My heart raced; my baby awoke and turned beneath my heart, and I knew that my stress was his in the weeks before his birth.

When he was born, my son startled at everything: the vacuum cleaner; our friend who had a cough; a car roaring by outside. My child had been primed into having an overactive stress response by his mother. So, the question is, can this be undone?"

A good story is supposed to keep you reading – so we will come back to that question at the end of the book.

The immediate environments surrounding our babies in utero and our children after birth have a role to play in how children's brains and nervous systems develop.

What we do as parents has a real effect on our children. Even if we are confronted with events that make our hearts race and prime our unborn children to have an overactive stress response, we can still do so much that will benefit them and their futures. We can make choices, create the spaces that give them the best chance of living happy, healthy lives.

Interestingly, we tend to glamourise stress. When we tell people how stressed we are, it somehow earns us badges – people view us as "overachievers" and therefore somehow "successful", "driven". If we're that stressed, we must be good people, who "give it our all".

Do we transfer this inherent belief to our children? As parents, we are usually very conscious of the environment surrounding our babies in their first weeks and months of life, but as they grow older, it's easy to lose sight of the fact that our implicit and explicit reactions to the world are shaping their responses. Our bodies were not designed for long-term fight-or-flight. They are wisely primed to respond appropriately to immediate threats and to get us away from that threat (mobilise glucose, direct blood away from the brain to the limbs so we can escape, speed up heart rate), and if we are in such a state chronically, this affects our health, our ability to respond to our children in a measured way, and their health – for the long-term.

As parents, being chronically stressed offers no advantages to us or our kids. It also sets us up for disease. Our first stop, then, is our own parental stress-response. We need to manage ourselves. Taking particular care of our stress-response puts us in the best position to not only respond to the stresses of parenting but also support our own physical, emotional and mental health.

Society has changed radically in the past 20 years. Technology offers us many efficient ways of being – of communicating, working, studying, travelling. But we'd like to propose the idea that getting faster and more efficient does not mean that every aspect of our lives improves. Some don't. And some valuable things get left on the roadside.

And sometimes, a freeway to the destination – whatever that might be – doesn't allow for any off-road exploration, which might actually lead to some of the most valuable discoveries of our lives.

There's a cost to the race towards a (shifting) end goal – whether it's about our children learning to walk, talk, play soccer, play the piano, learn maths, get into university, or get a well-paid job – and this is it: chronic, underlying stress/fear. Wait, there's more: the leading cause of death in developed countries is heart disease, and heart disease is directly linked to chronic stress.

However, if we become aware of the state of our hearts and bodies and take action in practical and time-tested ways, both we and our children may benefit exponentially.

As mentioned, we, as parents and caregivers, are the most important component of our children's immediate environment. Our physical, emotional and psychological state will impact our children, either positively or negatively. Also, our children's hearts and minds are shaped and impacted by the state of our own.

So What Is Stress?

Let's talk about stress. Or perhaps we should just call it "fear".

As a trained HeartMath Coach and Mentor with the Institute of HeartMath in California, Shelley has drawn from her work over several decades. This work focuses on mitigating the impact of stress for teachers and students in schools through restorative approaches to relationships using HeartMath Tools and the understanding of the autonomic nervous system to change our physiological, emotional and intellectual responses to stressful situations. Stress impacts our bodies, hearts and minds. It's essential that we prevent it from being a chronic factor in our and our children's lives.

Though stress is a wise physiological response to an immediate threat to our safety, it also *disrupts healthy physiological, emotional and cognitive function.*

Shelley grew up in Africa – a continent of apex predators. She's seen lions, leopards, crocodiles, and even people, sometimes, chase and take down prey. She has also had to run for her life; once from someone chasing her down a river when she was a child, and once when she was absolutely convinced there was a lion in the long, tawny grass. At that moment, walking through the golden waving veld, her heart rate went through the roof, blood drained from her face, her legs shook, and her stress response was mobilised so that she could get away. She ran, believing her life was in danger.

When she was finally able to breathe out, her heart rate slowed down. She looked back. No lion. Not this time. But there could have been. And her body had responded as if there had been. Now that she knew there was no lion, she breathed out. Her heart rate slowed – she felt relief, euphoria even. She could think clearly again.

This was a valid stress response to a potential threat to Shelley's life from an apex predator. And her autonomic nervous system worked perfectly.

Our autonomic nervous system is made up of the *sympathetic* nervous system (our fight-or-flight-or-freeze capacity), which speeds things up, and the *parasympathetic* nervous system, which slows everything down. Think: accelerator, brake. Everything's good when both work as they were designed to work. But of course, we're not mechanical – we're biological, emotional, psychological beings – so it's not as simple as having an "on/off" switch. What we can say, though, is that the sympathetic nervous system:

1. accelerates the heartbeat
2. stimulates secretion of stress hormones
3. causes a shift of blood supply towards the limbs and away from the brain.

While the parasympathetic nervous system:

1. slows the heartbeat
2. stops the secretion of stress hormones
3. directs blood-flow towards the brain.

We may know the difference intellectually between, say, a nasty comment from a friend or partner, and a lion in the grass, but our bodies have the same physical response to both of these stressors: our heart rates increase, blood flows away from our brains to our limbs, and stress hormones race through our systems. Our bodies don't differentiate between stressors that are actually "out there" and the ones that are in our minds. Imagine if we could see what was happening in our bodies and our children's bodies and brains throughout the day as we all respond to the things that happen around us. We'd probably change the way we do a few things.

For example, we may have a physiological response to an argument that almost equals being chased by a lion. And the longer and more frequently we have these responses, the more it becomes our baseline.

The important point here is that emotional and psychological states not only affect our bodies but also have a profound impact on our children – because we are the most important part of the home environment.

It's also worth knowing that our brains become familiar with certain patterns and default responses to those patterns, regardless of whether they are good for us or not. So, if we're primed to have a hugely stressful response to the world, that's our default position. It takes time and real effort to retrain our brains – but it can be done.

Our lives as parents are busy and it's easy to get stuck in overdrive – but imagine an accelerator that has jammed! That's what happens to our sympathetic nervous systems when we don't get to breathe out, and it's the recipe for parental burnout. When we're stressed, we often react too quickly, too aggressively, too fearfully. We've all heard our own voices shouting too loudly, "Stop shouting!" Yeah, exactly!

What Can We Do?

There are many ways of "breathing out" and taking simple, effective steps that support optimum autonomic nervous system functioning for parents and, by association, children. We can change the entire landscape of familial relationships by understanding that the first port of call is us: our bodies, our breath, our own nervous systems. Once we begin to understand how the stress response works, we have the opportunity to write a new script based on that new understanding for every challenging situation we might face, reducing the stress factor and making our lives more physically, psychologically and emotionally sustainable.

Let's face it. We can't control the way the world works, or the million different ways other people's decisions and actions affect us every day. We can't control the way our kids behave from moment to moment, but we always have a choice.

We can choose how we respond.

And the more we work on our own stress response, the more we can self-manage – and the more that will become our baseline.

For example, if we sit too long thinking about certain things – rising living costs, things we said that we wish we hadn't, jobs we've taken on that we feel we have no time for – we can easily set our hearts racing. Our palms get sweaty. Blood flows away from our brains to our limbs (but we're not going to get up and run away from those predators in our heads, so all those stress hormones will just keep on flowing through us). Pretty soon we will be pale, jittery, short-tempered and unable to respond in a measured way to even small stressors. And if we're not aware that this is happening, our brain will just keep reinforcing an overactive stress-response pathway.

It's understandable, then, that when we get caught in chronic "fight-or-flight" mode, we want something to throw us out of it. A glass of wine. A beer. Other things that will provide relief from our own runaway train of nervous energy. The predators that live in our imaginations often have nothing to fence them in or keep them under control. It's worse when we're feeling tired or stretched and we don't have the ability to stop that runaway train.

Too much adrenaline (epinephrine) is toxic. This is why we sometimes feel sick when we're afraid. Children who are frightened or stressed often complain of stomach aches and nausea. This is physical, not imaginary. Stress makes us feel sick.

You might think: it's all very well identifying the problem, but what can we do about this? How do we get ourselves off the stress-freeway and become that Zen parent who floats above the fray and smiles benevolently as chaos unfolds all around?

We don't think that parent exists – yet. But having the tools to begin creating a balanced autonomic nervous system allows us to be less reactive, and more able to create a sustainable, stress-proof (not stress-free!) environment. This in turn will support our kids.

Heart and Brain Connection!

For decades now, the Institute of HeartMath in California has been involved in in-depth research on how the state of our hearts affects our brains – and importantly, how our collective hearts interact with one another and affect one another.

Our hearts are constantly reacting to whatever is happening to us – they speed up and slow down – we feel stress, love, excitement and our hearts respond accordingly. Our hearts, in fact, generate an electromagnetic field that is measurable by sensitive magnetometers. When two people are at a conversational distance, each can detect the electromagnetic field of the other, and this has an effect on us. Someone who is very stressed can pull us into the same state. Likewise, someone who is calm and loving can have the opposite effect on someone else. Oxytocin (the love or bonding hormone), which is secreted by the pituitary gland, is also detectable in the heart.[7] Feeling love, it turns out, really happens in our hearts.

The latest research in neuroscience confirms that emotion and cognition can best be thought of as separate but interacting functions or systems, each with its unique intelligence. The research is showing that the key to the successful integration of the mind and emotions lies in increasing the coherence (ordered, harmonious function) in both systems and bringing them into phase with one another.

When we are full of the powerful emotions of love or gratitude, we generate an electromagnetic field that is more "coherent" than when we are feeling fear or anxiety. This has an effect on those around us, especially on our children.

According to the Institute of HeartMath, when we're stressed we set off a cascade of about 1400 neurobiological processes that are depleting – to save us from immediate danger. Likewise, feeling love and gratitude sets off a series of about 1400 neurobiological processes that are regenerative or renewing. So, being stressed is bad for us. It's also bad for our kids. Being able to manage stress, and better still, being able to generate a coherent, loving feeling benefits our own health and supports the kids we care for.

Our hearts inform our brains. Professor Rollin McCraty, lead researcher at the Institute of HeartMath, and his team of researchers maintain that heart-to-brain messages are twice as frequent as brain-to-heart messages.[8] This means that our hearts are the main detectors of what's happening in the environment. So, whatever our kids experience in their days – how we treat them, whether we're over-reactive or permissive or loving and supportive, whatever they're feeling – that will affect their autonomic nervous systems *and* their brains. The way we treat our kids – everything we say, everything we do – affects their nervous systems and ultimately is written into their neural circuitry.

Understanding what happens in our hearts and our nervous systems offers parents the first step to informing the decisions we make as our kids grow. We are the first port of call. And while a mother's womb is the first environment a child learns from, after that it's the home, and the people in the home, their voices, reactions, emotions. Beyond that, the wider world starts to have an impact, but focusing on the environment that we inhabit and create in the early years may lay the groundwork for later. We can either prime our kids to have overactive sympathetic nervous systems – or not. We don't know anyone who would choose the former.

Now that you have some understanding of stress and the nervous system, we can focus a bit more on the science underpinning this discussion. Heart rate variability (HRV) is the name we give to the beat-to-beat variations in our heart rhythms. Unless you have a pacemaker, your heart doesn't keep exact time. It speeds up and slows down in minuscule ways according to every event you experience, and a person who can adapt well to change usually has *high* variability. This is true of children and babies too. High variability is correlated with adaptability. Kids with low variability often exhibit behaviour issues; any kind of change acts as a stressor, because they can't adapt quickly enough to new conditions.

Try this experiment: with your finger on your pulse, breathe in and out slowly. When does your pulse speed up, and when does it slow down?

You're right if you noticed that heart rate speeds up when you inhale and slows when you exhale. That's the sympathetic nervous system at work when you breathe in, and the parasympathetic nervous system kicking in when you breathe out. Accelerator. Brake.

When we sigh, or hear kids sighing, that's the wise body trying to kick the parasympathetic nervous system into gear so the accelerator doesn't get stuck. Slow down that racing heart. Stop fretting. Our bodies are brilliant and know what to do.

Heart rate variability, which can be measured by an echocardiogram, is a measurement of naturally occurring beat-to-beat changes in heart rate. *HRV patterns are extremely responsive to emotions, and heart rhythms tend to become more ordered, or coherent, during positive emotional states.*[9]

Enough about stress now. Let's look at what happens when we're in a positive emotional state. The results can be life-changing in the short-term and also in the long-term – for us and our kids.

When we're feeling positive and happy, our heart rhythms become more ordered, more harmonious. If we hold our babies and love them, and talk to them, they experience that positive emotional state which then affects the growing brain's electrical activity. This is a form of attachment that is integral to all aspects of development and supported by a plethora of research studies. It is also something that literally gets imprinted on our neural circuitry. This isn't new news, but much of our children's neural patterning is already inherent long before they'd ever remember the experiences that informed those patterns.[10] Moreover, these patterns play an important role in fostering a variety of emotional states.

Let's look at one definition of a positive emotional state: the Institute of HeartMath defines a state of "high coherence" as an optimal, measurable state of balance, harmony and integration between our hearts, our brains, and the rest of our bodies: "Psychophysiological coherence... involves a high degree of balance, harmony and synchronization within and between cognitive, emotional and physiological processes. Research has shown that this state is associated with high performance, reduced stress, increased emotional stability and numerous health benefits."[11]

We know this intuitively, but understanding that a positive emotional state affects our physical health in a measurable way, and by association our children's health, is an important starting point for being "grounded" in our approaches to parenting.

A high state of coherence means that the person experiencing it is in a state of balance. Look at the heart rhythm patterns below. The heart rhythms of someone who is feeling frustrated look sharp, jagged, uneven. In contrast, the heart rhythms of a person feeling love, gratitude and appreciation create the flowing sine wave that represents the optimum state of "high coherence".[12]

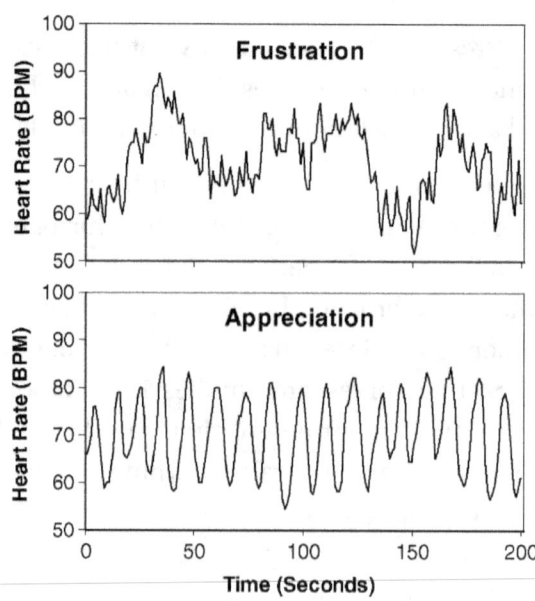

Professor Rollin McCraty states in *The Coherent Heart* that "When positive emotions are used to shift the heart's pattern of activity into coherence, a global transformation in psychophysiological function occurs... this transformation results in increased physiological efficiency, greater emotional stability, and enhanced cognitive function and performance."[13]

Children who are chronically exposed to stress are disadvantaged. Their growing bodies and brains are affected negatively, and they end up primed for fight-or-flight. The good news is that we as parents have a powerful capacity to create an environment that supports them by working on ourselves. It does take effort. But the moment we become aware that our emotions and our bodies are our most powerful allies in providing our kids with the support they need, the job of "doing things right" as parents becomes easier. An environment with a loving and coherent parent or two can help children to experience high coherence; and ordered, harmonious heart rhythm patterns reflect enhanced cognitive function. Supporting our kids to feel happy and loved and *un*stressed is also the best way to make them smarter. Imagine that!

Ground Rules

1. The environment surrounding newborn babies affects their neurological development.
2. What happens in our hearts influences our brain's electrical activity.
3. "High coherence" is an optimum state.
4. Sustained positive emotional states have a positive effect on cognitive function.
5. Our children benefit in every way from being in a positive supportive environment.

Three

This Is Your Brain on Adolescence!

"Normal adolescence has its share of abnormal behaviour. The point bears repeating because it gets at the essence of why adolescence can be so difficult for kids themselves and the people around them. After all, how do you deal with a 'normally abnormal' time of life?"

– Dr David Walsh[14]

Living in a Storm of Raging Hormones!

How do you deal with a normally abnormal time of life? Have you ever wondered why the transition out of childhood towards adulthood can be so challenging and seemingly abnormal? So many things change when a child enters, and moves through, adolescence. To help you better understand this, we would like to provide some clarity around the term "adolescence".

Adolescence means many things to many people, depending on culture and context. For our purposes, and as a starting point, adolescence is best linked to the term "pubescence". Pubescence is a medical term denoting a change in the reproductive capacities of an individual. In other words, adolescence is a period of life when a child is transitioning into someone who can produce offspring. With this transition, the body will start to change its shape, hormones will impact physiology and behaviour, and children will begin to grow into young men and women. It is noteworthy that pubescence also signals the beginning of changes to the brain, and as such, phrases like the "teen brain" are not quite accurate, given that some children enter puberty long before their thirteenth birthday. Therefore, we use the word adolescence as an umbrella term that spans roughly the "tweens" (10–12) and "teens" (13–18) years.

Given all the changes briefly noted, is it any wonder that adolescence has its share of abnormal behaviours? These behaviours range from changes to sleep patterns and moods, to novelty and sensation-seeking activities or what you might call experimentation, to grunting as a form of communication, and to risk-taking and all its inherent outcomes, be they positive or negative. Perhaps this is why one of the most influential psychologists of the 20th century, G. Stanley Hall, described adolescence as a "heightened time of storm and stress".[15]

With all of the changes to the bodies and minds of adolescents, it should not come as any surprise that this time of life is one where anxiety and stress, as Hall suggested, can flourish. And because adolescence is a critical period of significant brain maturation and reconstruction, the world surrounding adolescents as they mature can contribute to a number of mental health issues. However, there are also opportunities to calm the storm and by association support the changes noted in a positive manner. In order to unpack how that can be achieved, a bit more neuroscientific understanding beyond that discussed in Chapter 1 is necessary.

The Adolescent Brain, or Lack Thereof!

In Chapter 1 you were introduced to the early stages of brain development and the role of experiences in shaping the neuro-circuitry of the brain. It was also noted that the brain actually sets up more neural connections than are needed, and how myelin is so important for neurons to create synaptic connections. During adolescence, brain circuits are defined more sharply, with new synapses being added in a sea of increased myelin growth. At the same time, unused connections are discarded – or "pruned" as neuroscientists say – while many other connections are strengthened. Even as the teenage years end, the brain is still fine-tuning itself. The prefrontal lobes, the centre of planning and decision-making, won't mature fully until the mid-twenties, which is why you can see frequent risk-taking and poor judgement displayed by some from their late teens through to their early twenties.

An 18-year-old student of one of the authors thought nothing of tying himself with a rope to the back of a friend's ute and riding full speed on his skateboard behind the ute as it drove downhill in the middle of the night on a dark country road. This didn't go well, and he ended up in hospital. He couldn't make sense of his decision to pull the stunt after the fact. He could not answer his parents' questions of why – why did you do such a ridiculous thing?

Responding to a parent's desire to know why something like this was done does not come easy for those whose brains are still working to become more mature and sophisticated. It takes time for those connections to develop that give a developing brain the wherewithal to gain meaningful control over emotional impulse or poor decision-making and think through the consequences of one's actions. That's the big picture, but there are some important considerations regarding the developing brain during adolescence that deserve a bit more discussion.

As noted earlier, during adolescence the brain undergoes a massive remodelling of its basic structures. This occurs in regions of the brain that effect everything from logic and language to impulses and empathy. During this remodelling, and as alluded to above, myelin, the brain's white matter, will increase about 100 percent in volume in order to help the brain become more efficient in passing information from one neuron to another. At the same time as that myelin is increasing, the brain is also being deconstructed – or perhaps "renovated" is a better term. Essentially, it is getting rid of unused synaptic connections or pruning itself to become more refined.

The pruning of synapses is an amazing neurological journey where the brain eliminates those connections associated with actions, activities and/or experiences that are no longer practised or important and strengthens the connections that are repeatedly activated. Remember the "use it or lose it" principle we discussed in Chapter 1? Well, during adolescence this process is a key factor in shaping the minds of young people.

Please remember this: it is the environment and interactions within it that shape an adolescent's neural superhighway.

Perhaps you should highlight the preceding sentence, as it is immensely important when we look at what might be shaping the brain, given that adolescents are sometimes referred to as "screenagers"! More on that a bit later.

Now, amidst all of the restructuring and pruning, it is important to remember that the brain matures roughly from the bottom up and around to the front and from the inside out. Maturation has different timelines for different areas and occurs at different rates for males and females. This maturational process is apparent in some very important regions of the brain associated with rewards, emotions and emotional regulation, which in turn impact on thinking – or the lack thereof – and behaviour. We could get quite technical and discuss things like the nucleus accumbens and other structures, but instead let's focus on how some of the systems in the brains of adolescents differ from yours.

First, let's remember that the brain's CEO, the frontal lobes, don't fully mature until we are in our twenties. So, the part of the brain that you use to make responsible decisions, pay attention to things, evaluate rewards, regulate emotions, consider the feelings of others, and many other important functions, is not working as well in adolescents. The adolescent brain is more primal and views the world and what happens in it through emotion and survival. It is also geared to look for novel experiences and sensation-seeking activities and to take risks. Major contributors to adolescent thrill-seeking are changes in the brain's reward systems and a powerful neurotransmitter called dopamine.

Neurotransmitters are the chemical messengers between synapses, and dopamine is often referred to as "the pleasure chemical". When you turn on your radio and hear a song you love, your dopamine will elevate about 10 percent, dance merrily in your brain's reward circuits, and make you feel good. Dopamine can also be elevated by sweet and salty foods, drugs, exercise, sex, healthy relationships and risk-taking and can impact thinking, memory, moods, sleep, attention, concentration, movement and motivation. You can see that it is a very important player in our behaviours, especially when we are motivated to get a reward.

Rewards are important to us! People will never complain about receiving a reward, but for adolescents, things are a bit different. Dopamine seems to be exceedingly elevated in the adolescent brain's reward centres, leaving them with an incessant desire to feel good. And because an adolescent's frontal lobes are still developing, they will look for immediate rewards for the least amount of effort and without much thought of consequences. This is why adolescents tend to prefer activities that require relatively low effort yet produce high excitement, such as playing video games, skateboarding, risk- and sensation-seeking and experimenting with tobacco, alcohol or other substances. This need for excitement may also be influenced by structures in the brain that process emotion and ensure our survival.

There are two tiny almond-shaped structures called the amygdala, tucked deep into the brain, which help us respond emotionally to a range of experiences. As an adult, you are in a position to think clearly about and/or override any messages from these structures because your brain's CEO can put the brakes on them. This is not something that adolescents can do very well. For example, one of the reasons why adolescents are moody is that they are more likely to overreact to a negative situation because of an immature amygdala. It is the amygdala that is responsible for automatic "hot" responses rather than the "cool" considered responses of the frontal lobes. Interestingly, an immature amygdala means adolescents will often see anger in faces when there isn't any and get their backs up in preparation to survive what they assume is some kind of hostile attack. In the end, it is not terribly uncommon for adolescents to feel that they live in a hostile and dangerous world, and their responses to this world are not always well considered, kind or gentle. You may be smiling, but they may see a threat. These feelings can also be manifested as anxiety and stress, which we will look at in more detail shortly.

By now, it should be clear that the developmental changes in the brain noted earlier are responsible for transforming a child into a restless, exuberant and emotionally intense adolescent. Understandably, there are enormous challenges associated with supporting, nurturing and guiding adolescents. And while every older generation bemoans the plight of adolescents or the current generation of young people, it could be argued that today's adolescents face cultural and social changes unlike previous generations. Worryingly, young people appear to have fewer opportunities to do the types of activities that their grandparents experienced and instead spend a great deal of time in a media-rich, 24/7, socially monitored virtual world.

Remember: *experiences matter!* Prior to the turn of the century, adolescent experiences were not usually happening virtually. Sure, young people may have been at arcades playing video games, but for the most part they were going to movies, hanging out with friends, playing sports, going on first dates, going shopping or doing many other things that they likely cajoled their parents into letting them do. Then, of course, there were those things that were hidden from parents as adolescents took risks and experimented with tobacco or alcohol, skipped school, and found ways of doing things that would make their younger siblings cringe in disbelief. All of these experiences, whether sanctioned by parents or not, were important in shaping a young person's identity and building independence from Mum and/or Dad. It was part of "growing up" and learning, and we all did it!

Part of growing up is learning to make better decisions by making not-so-good decisions, or becoming better planners by making plans, implementing them and evaluating the results, again and again. For previous generations, growing up was mostly about friends and doing things in real time. Those experiences were, and still are, incredibly important for healthy development. This is the interplay between nature and nurture; the brain matures and learns within the environment around it. As noted earlier, it is concerning that today's adolescents are growing up in a very different environment than previous generations of young people.

The Adolescent Brain in the 21st Century

Let's start this section by reiterating that nature and nurture work in tandem to shape the brain. That dance between what's inside our skull and the world around it has evolved over many millennia. We would contend, however, that the turn of the century began ushering in a vast new array of experiences – namely, the advent of technology and screen devices in the lives of young and old alike. Sure, there were computers prior to the year 2000, but for many decades computers were not "personal", nor were they easy to use.

Some of you may remember a time when having a computer was not the norm. It was not until sometime in the 1980s that computers began to show up in people's homes. It wasn't until 1983 that the first "laptop" was marketed and until the 1990s that many people were learning to live with, and eventually for, computers. By the turn of the century, personal computers of varying shapes and sizes had become commonplace. This also coincided with the emergence of the world wide web or internet and the exponential growth in access to information. Today, about 90 percent of western children under the age of four are familiar with how to use various screens, while the majority of adolescents have their own smartphones.

There are some who might think that having a phone is no big deal really. Maybe! But this does not take into account two things that we have outlined here and in Chapter 1. The first of these is recognising that the brain does not fully mature until we are well into our third decade of life. The second is that during adolescence the brain is being reconstructed under a "use it or lose it" process. Combined, this means that the adolescent brain is a perfect organ for having its mind shaped by experiences – remember experience-dependent growth?

Some years ago, the U.S. Public Broadcasting Service's "Frontline" TV program presented a special episode on the "teen" brain. During this program, and commenting on the process of synaptic pruning, Jay Giedd, Professor of Neuroscience and Psychiatry at the University of California, San Diego, stated:

> "If an adolescent is doing music, sports or academics, those are the connections that will be hard wired. If they're lying on the couch or playing video games or watching MTV, those are the cells and connections that are going to survive."

This statement encapsulates one of the most worrying aspects of the experiences that adolescents, and children for that matter, are deeply immersed in. Being on a screen for extended periods of time, by many current measures, is not only unhealthy but might also be shaping the brain in ways that are detrimental to overall development and mental health. Research across several disciplines has identified that screen devices and the virtual worlds that are found through them are negatively impacting on everything from body posture to eye problems to addiction to behavioural problems and an array of mental health issues. Screen devices are also central to something referred to as a "displacement hypothesis".

The term displacement hypothesis sounds rather technical, but it really just asks this question: while kids are attached to a phone, what aren't they doing? This is an important consideration during both the early years of life and adolescence. When an infant or toddler is using or being "babysat" by a smartphone, they aren't looking at other people around them, smiling, trying to get attention, or observing the faces and behaviours of anyone around them – all actions and interactions that are vital for learning and healthy development. The same holds true for adolescents who spend more time in a virtual world than a real one. They miss opportunities for honing their cognitive, emotional and social skill sets.

Honing the skill sets is an important component of adolescent development, and this occurs in real time with other people. The social milieu and engagement with peers, family, friends and adults alike help shape the adolescent brain. This is the story of development in countless generations but something that is being interrupted by today's technology. Young people are spending more and more time on screen devices, and we have now moved beyond trying to work out what amount of time constitutes healthy screen use. Instead, we must consider shifting the balance between screens and real-time interactions and experiences, and for good reason.

Enter Screen Environments with Caution

It may surprise you to know that, prior to the turn of the century, most research showed a consistent increase in aspects of psychological well-being in younger populations. Adolescents, in particular, were showing net positives in measures of happiness, self-esteem and life satisfaction.[16] Young people were happy and thriving. Then something interesting started to emerge when our calendars moved into the 21st century: the measures showing increases in positive aspects of mental health in young people started to show a steady decline. This decline then began to fall precipitously from 2007. Coincidently, 2007 is when the first Apple iPhone hit the marketplace, and since that time it has become ubiquitous among children and teens.

Now, there will be some people unwilling to entertain the thought of screen devices being a mental health hazard, but we are not those people. Our research and writing strongly correlates screen use with declines in many aspects of healthy development.[17] Those who would disagree with us often say that there is a difference between correlation and causation, and we agree. However, a bit of discussion will help you, the reader, understand why we must rely on correlation and how the data continues to support our position.

Let's start with imagining you are on a committee that decides whether researchers can do some experiments based on whether those experiments have any potential for harming the participants; in other words, you are deciding the "ethics" of the proposed study. A proposal is then submitted whereby the researchers are going to use children as their participants. In the study, some of the children will be exposed to hours of activities on smartphones and observed to see how long they can be on those devices before measurable harm occurs, and this will be collected as data. Would you give permission for such a study? Probably not, and for good reason: it is unethical to conduct research that has the potential to do harm. However, while we cannot do experiments that harm students, that does not mean that correlational studies that speak to potential harms can be discounted. It is our contention that the growing volume of studies that correlate screen usage and declines in mental health is ample proof that something is not right. There is no doubt that the mental health of adolescents has seen sharp declines with corresponding increases in screentime. The burden of proof for anyone suggesting otherwise is to present data indicating the contrary to what we note rather than harping on about whether a study proves causation.

There has been an exponential growth in studies suggesting that screen devices are doing more harm than good when left unchecked. The last part of that sentence is the important part for parents. We would never suggest that young people should not have access to screen devices, as that is simply unrealistic. What we are suggesting is that parents should become grounded in the knowledge that the environment plays a role in shaping the brains and minds of adolescents. The current environment also creates the need for parents to be grounded in knowing that screen devices have issues and challenges and that having a phone is not a rite of passage for your child, nor is it something your child should assume will happen or something to be taken for granted.

Something to be aware of is that even while teenagers are lying almost immobile on the couch with nothing more than a few fingers twitching, whatever they are watching, playing or engaging with on screen is having a real physiological effect: hearts are speeding up and slowing down. There's adrenaline, cortisol, dopamine. Depending on the nature of the virtual reality, the activity could be creating addictive patterning, heightening the stress-response, or amplifying a sense of not being good enough or missing out on the fun others are having.

As researchers and authors, we have spoken on this subject to many parents and also to many students. One of the responses we often get to our concerns is something to the effect that: if my child does not have a phone or their time is limited on screen devices, they will not be able to be part of their friend group or they may be left out. Does that sound familiar? Is there a chance that this argument has preceded this generation? How many generations of adolescents have told their parents that if they don't have something they will not fit in? From sneakers to hairstyles to cars, and now phones, young people have a long history of decrying the perceived injustices of having to go without something they consider essential. What we have seen in recent times, however, is parents making that argument on behalf of their children. We believe they do so with all manner of good intentions and only want their children to fit in and be happy. However, aside from the myriad of mental health issues linked with screen devices discussed earlier, perhaps the following anecdote will help calm parents' minds.

In research conducted as a pilot study just prior to the pandemic, over 1300 high school students across Australia and New Zealand took part in a survey focusing on smartphone usage. In one part of that survey, 1372 students identified that smartphones were contributing factors to the following issues in their lives:

- Tiredness/poor sleep (91%)
- Inactivity/sedentary behaviour (65%)
- Decline in school grades (64%)
- Reduction in social activity (63%)
- Anxiety (58%)
- Attention problems (56%)
- Depression (56%)

There are some interesting points to be made before the real bombshell is dropped. The students were not coached or given any information related to issues around smartphones other than multiple-choice questions as part of the survey. They in turn identified issues that are evident in the types of research studies we have mentioned, including those linked to mental health – anxiety and depression.

We found this to be interesting and compelling, but even more interesting was what we heard when we did follow-up interviews with a large number of willing students. One of the things that the students told us was that, while they were well aware of the issues noted, they were unwilling to make any changes related to their use of and behaviours associated with smartphones. This was not terribly surprising given their still-developing brains, their desire for risk-taking, sensation-seeking and novelty, or their sense of peer pressure and influence. What was surprising was when they told us that, while they weren't going to voluntarily change, they would be happy for their parents to set boundaries and guidelines for all screen time. This makes sense! An adolescent is unlikely to tell their peers and friends that they heard about the types of issues we are speaking of or read studies about the perils of smartphones and so decided to curtail their phone use – that would not be cool! They would, however, happily blame their parents for monitoring their use, engaging in some form of digital detox, or even "de-phoning" them if need be. It's easier to tell your friends that your parents are cruel Luddites than to admit you are concerned about phones and taking steps voluntarily.[18]

This brings us to one last point before closing this chapter. Many people are under the impression that peers are the most important influence in the lives of adolescents. Peers are certainly important, but research literature also tells us that the most significant person in the life of an adolescent is an adult role model, and most of the time that is Mum and/or Dad! So, parents, rest assured, you do have significant influence in the lives of your adolescent children, even when they seem to be pushing back on all you say and do. They need to push back to help them become independent and shape their identity as they move into adulthood. But do not underestimate your important role in shaping their environment for them to thrive. You play a significant part in grounding your adolescent children in the real world and parenting the virtual world.

Ground Rules

1. The adolescent brain is a work in progress, so don't let a teen's physical size fool you – they are not miniature adults.

2. Adolescents are primed for rewards, sensation-seeking and risk-taking, and as such your guidance and expectations must be forthright and consistent.

3. It is important to monitor and regulate screen use to ensure healthy development.

4. Social media has been linked to a substantial number of problems during adolescence and as such also needs to be monitored.

5. Adolescents are driven by emotions and sometimes appear to lack any measure of logical and responsible thinking; however, always stay positive and look for what is strong with your teen rather than what is wrong with them.

Four

Focus on Resilience Instead of Trauma

> "When people are traumatised, especially early in life, their defences and assumptions of safety are prematurely shattered... The silver lining is that traumatic experiences are also capable of enhancing self-discovery and often support the attainment of wisdom."
>
> – Dr Louis Cozolino[19]

The Impact of Trauma

Simon had panic attacks at school from the time he was seven until he was twelve. His heart would race, he would feel like he was dying, and he had to go to the office where his parents were notified and came to pick him up. The attacks started soon after his family had a near-fatal car accident.

The boy's trauma impacted his ability to function at school, and he missed out on a lot. His nervous system was in overdrive, and he could not get himself out of fight-or-flight mode. That's when he learned a biofeedback technique which involved nothing more than breathing in and out for five or six seconds each time, focusing on a feeling of love or appreciation for something or someone, and doing this several times a day – sometimes during a panic attack, sometimes in the morning or before bed. This technique, termed the "Quick Coherence Technique" by the Institute of HeartMath, allowed him to bring his autonomic nervous system into balance. After months of doing this, Simon was able to manage his panic attacks better as they happened. Nervous system balance leads to emotional, physiological and psychological balance. And vice versa.[20] He built a new physiological baseline.

The anecdote earlier sets the framework for the next couple of chapters. We are hoping to give you greater insights into a topic that has gained much exposure and attention over the last few years, namely trauma. We also want to assure you that there are things you can do and things that are best left out of classrooms and school environments.

Let's begin this discussion by recognising that trauma – not too dissimilar to stress – is a physiological response to a situation that impacts the intricate connections between the heart, brain and body. However, we would argue that the use of the word "trauma" is not always appropriate in all circumstances. To help understand this, a bit of background information is necessary.

While it could be argued that we have always been interested in how certain negative life events impact on children, research in this area has grown exponentially since the turn of the century. It was at that time that the phrase "Adverse Childhood Experiences" or ACEs first originated from a groundbreaking study involving almost 14,000 participants in the United States. The study basically looked at the relationships between childhood trauma and various risk factors for leading causes of death among those adults who had experienced trauma as children. It should come as no surprise that the study found a strong relationship between the breadth and type of exposure to trauma during childhood and multiple risk factors for several of the leading causes of death among adults.[21] Importantly, the ACEs identified included psychological, physical, or sexual abuse; violence against the mother; and living with household members who were substance abusers, mentally ill or suicidal, or had been imprisoned. Again, it was not surprising that those types of experiences might have an impact on a child as they matured into adulthood.

Now you may be wondering why we are laying out the history and our growing understanding of the nature and extent of ACEs. From the research noted, then, there has been a growth of interventionist measures across numerous sectors for helping children who might be at risk of being traumatised. Given that you are reading a book on parenting, we highly doubt that your children are at risk from the types of challenges noted, but they may find themselves having to deal with traumatic events, and they will need your help to do so.

Before unpacking what you can do to support yourself and your children, it is worth considering things to avoid. As authors, and also as long-time parents and educators, we are aware of the pernicious nature of both stress and trauma and how they have spawned a cottage industry of experts ready to help your child. We don't want to sound too negative, but the tendency to try to "fix" children has become commonplace in western society and permeated many institutions, including schools. Indeed, schools today are increasingly engaging in professional development sessions to embed "trauma-informed practice" into their day-to-day operations. Right now, you might be asking yourself: is that such a bad thing? Allow us to offer some food for thought.

It goes without saying that we believe schools should be safe places for children to thrive, grow, learn and succeed in. It is also true that teachers can provide comfort and support to young people in need. After all, as mentioned in the introduction, teachers are expected to embrace the Latin phrase *in loco parentis* or "in the place of parents". That is not to say that teachers literally take the place of parents, but when children arrive at school there is an underlying expectation that teachers will provide the safety and care that would be found in the home. We contend that teachers, by and large, do this intuitively, without hesitation and rather subconsciously. For this, we salute schools and their staff. However, we would like to offer a few words of caution.

A Cautionary Tale

To start this cautionary tale, let's revisit what is broadly meant when we talk about stress, trauma and young people, especially children. As you may recall from previous chapters, the brain is a work in progress that takes more than two decades to fully mature, so your child's brain and nervous system are more vulnerable to the impacts of stress and trauma. Stress and trauma are therefore not great for children in terms of overall healthy development. However, not all stress is bad, nor traumatic.

Professor John Shonkoff and colleagues at Harvard University's Centre on the Developing Child offer a concise framework for understanding stress. This framework helps us to understand that not all stress is bad, but some sources of stress can certainly lead to trauma. Stress can take three forms: *positive, tolerable* and *toxic*.[22]

Positive stress is a normal and necessary part of healthy development. This is the type of stress that might occur on a child's first day of school or first immunisation or when a student might have to do a public speech. Researchers refer to positive stress as "eustress" and see it as an important adaptive mechanism for building resilience. It is characterised by brief increases in heart rate and mild elevations of some hormones and easily attended to in supportive environments with the help of stable relationships – usually those with parents and caregivers but also with teachers.

Tolerable and toxic stress are different. These stressors can have a very negative impact on the developing brain and body if not attended to with care. Tolerable stress activates the brain's alert systems when we experience more severe or longer-lasting difficulties. The loss of a loved one, a frightening injury, parental divorce or family break-up, a natural disaster or community violence are all examples of tolerable stress. They are tolerable because such events are often time limited and buffered by adults who help the child adapt and cope so that the brain and other organs recover as quickly as possible to avoid long-term negative effects.

Toxic stress is the worst and least desirable of the three. It can occur when a child experiences strong, frequent and prolonged adversity in the forms of physical or emotional abuse, exposure to violence, chronic neglect, caregiver substance abuse and/or mental illness, to name a few. In these situations, the brain is hyper-vigilant towards ensuring survival, flooding the body with all kinds of stress hormones and chemicals and potentially disrupting all manner of development. Toxic stress can last a lifetime. It is the type of stress that helped shape our understanding of ACEs noted earlier. It has been linked to heart disease, diabetes, anxiety disorders, substance abuse and depression, but once again, caring adults as early in life as possible are the best buffer for preventing or reversing the damaging effects of toxic stress.

The descriptions of stress may appear somewhat clinical, so let us unpack this further with some anecdotes that might help you better understand what trauma is, what it is not, and how it can be so impactful in the life of a young person. For example, let's consider children who grow up in regions of the world where there is continuous conflict. One of us, Shelley, can speak personally to this, given her years growing up in South Africa during Apartheid. At that time, South Africa had a high level of societal violence (which continues to this day), with generational trauma that is ongoing. Many children have seen family members being killed in front of them. This is a type of trauma which one may never completely recover from or adequately process without help. Moreover, the ability to be able to function as a resilient member of society is impeded when seriously traumatic events happen to you as a child.

The type of trauma noted earlier is a deep and profound injury that can last a lifetime and often results in a variety of mental health disorders including Post Traumatic Stress Disorder (PTSD).

So severe is this type of trauma that it can be passed down to future generations, as evidenced in the science of epigenetics.

Without getting bogged down in technical terms, epigenetics looks at how a person's behaviours, experiences and/or environment can cause changes that affect the way their genes work. So powerful is the connection between experiences and genes, researchers at Emory University were able to instil fear in future generations of mice.[23]

In this study, scientists taught male mice to fear the smell of cherry blossoms by linking that smell to mild foot shocks. Basically, every time a mouse was exposed to the scent of cherry blossoms, it was given an electrical shock. Those mice eventually developed a heightened stress-response to the smell, even when the shocks were not given. Not long after being conditioned in this way, the mice bred with females. The newborn pups were then raised into adulthood having never been exposed to the smell of cherry blossoms. However, when they caught a whiff of cherry blossom for the very first time, they became anxious and fearful. That fear had been passed down genetically. Wait, there's more!

The scientists also found that the fearful mice were born with more cherry blossom-detecting sensors in their noses and more brain space devoted to cherry blossom smelling. The memory transmission and fear response they received extended out another generation when these male mice bred and similar results were found in their pups. Think of that carefully. Trauma-induced physiological changes were not only passed on to the children of the shocked mice but also to their grandchildren. We will return to these amazing findings later in the chapter when we discuss how you must ensure, to the best of your ability, that you do not pass on stress and/or trauma to your children or potentially to a yet-unborn child and grandchild.

Now that you have been equipped with more information about trauma, it should be easy to see the differences between stress and trauma and how stress can become trauma. The first day of school is one thing, but continued exposure to violence, be it in the home or in a war-torn country, is something very different. That being said, it might surprise you to know that some forms of trauma can be the result of doing things too early, before children are ready – emotionally, psychologically or physically – to do what they're being asked to do. Anything that is not at the right time creates stress. When this happens repeatedly, the result is trauma. When the trauma is constantly brought up and talked about and amplified, it becomes more entrenched. Here are some examples of doing things at the wrong time.

We all walk and run if we have two legs and are able-bodied. But we know that a three-month-old infant is not in any way ready to walk or to run. They need to crawl first, and crawling leads to many positive neurological and structural benefits as a child moves from infancy into toddlerhood. To try to compel a child whose body and bones are soft and who is not even yet crawling to walk would likely create severe physical trauma and potentially lifelong emotional and psychological damage. Yet, some parents may embark on this journey under some misguided notion of advancing their children's skill set as soon as possible. Trying to do too much too soon can end up leading to less.

This also applies to introducing academic ideas or concepts that children are not ready to process yet. For example, children do not need to be literate when they enter their first year of school. The precursor to school success is good oral language skills and not the capacity to write one's name at four or five years of age. Relatedly, if we ask a six-year-old to write a persuasive piece, they are not developmentally anywhere near being able to process this. Their brains are too immature to understand and perform this task. They do not have a prefrontal cortex that is in any way equipped to process this kind of information, so being required to do something like this would create enormous stress, potentially resulting in trauma.

Now you might be doubting that such things really do happen in schools or homes, but you would be wrong. There are examples of schools doing the right things at the wrong time, facilitated by misguided bureaucracies and overzealous parents. Furthermore, the extent to which schools engage in alleviating trauma in children should be carefully monitored. It is our considered and collective professional opinion that obtaining a university degree in education and the associated qualifications for being a teacher is not a licence for acting as a therapist. Schooling and therapy can sometimes become intertwined in an effort to care, protect and nurture. However, creating a wholesome, supportive and – yes – even healing environment, does not equate with attempting to provide expert psychological intervention to traumatised children. In fact, there may even be things occurring in schools that *contribute* to stress and trauma in children and teens. We would do well to question if – under the good intentions of caring for young people – we are actually amplifying, exacerbating and pathologising trauma among children. We must also ask if media, government bureaucracies and schools are contributing to anxiety, stress and trauma among children and teens.

We unpack this in more depth in the next chapter, as there is much to discuss. For now, however, we wish to reiterate that any situation involving a stressed or traumatised child requires a response grounded in love and support from parents first and foremost. Certainly, other caregivers and teachers have a part to play, but that is only in lieu of bad, absent or toxic parenting, which is not what this book is about. We are simply trying to emphasise that you, as a parent, are the buffer between stress and trauma and your child, and with that come some personal responsibilities necessary to ensure that children like Simon, who opened this chapter, are supported most effectively.

One of the first things to always remember is that, as much as possible, you should keep your own nervous system balanced. Children have an uncanny ability to feel the stress of their parents. If you are struggling with some aspect of life, as we all do from time to time, you need to ensure you don't transfer those feelings to your children. Children who witness anxiety or stress in their parents can get caught up in those feelings and mirror them in similar situations.

Remember also what epigenetics tells us: children of anxious or stressed parents are more likely to exhibit anxiety themselves and be susceptible to all the negative side effects associated with anxiety and stress.

We are well aware that prescribing calm in the eye of any storm has many variables to consider, given the uniqueness of each human being. We do know, however, that there are some things you can do to ground yourself, alleviate your stress and set positive examples for your children.

Plan Ahead and Be Proactive

Part of being human is recognising and accepting that life can be difficult at times. That should be motivation enough for engaging in whatever activities you can to help buffer the mental duress that comes when challenges arise. Eating well, exercising and sleeping well are three foundational components of combating stress. Professor Bruce McEwan was a pioneer and one of the world's leading authorities on stress and combating stress. He made a habit of reminding people that diet, sleep and exercise are interconnected and integral to not only physical health but also mental health. Eat well and you tend to do more and sleep better; exercise regularly and you tend to eat nutritious food and sleep better; ensure you are doing all you can to have a restful sleep and you will have more energy to exercise and tend to eat better... we think you get the idea. When one of these is lacking, the others are impacted, so it is important to find a balance of the three that works for you.

While you lock in healthy exercise, eating and sleep habits, you might also consider activities that promote calming the mind. Yoga, meditation, mindfulness and breathwork programs all promote healthy consciousness and free the mind from stress. There are a variety of means of engaging with each of these types of activities, and you should choose what suits you and your lifestyle best. This is important when you consider that our brains and minds are so powerful that we can set off our fight-or-flight response by just imagining ourselves in threatening situations.[24] In other words, finding ways to switch off your mind is not only healthy but also therapeutic.

Another way to be proactive in combating stress is to identify and pay attention to what might trigger your stress response or anxiety. We can all feel anxious at times, but we make things worse if we spend too much time dwelling on it or jumping to worst-case scenarios. For example, the news cycle rarely shares positive news stories, so if the news makes you anxious then stop watching. Spend time reading, exercising or doing any of the mindful activities noted earlier, and avoid anything you think might arouse your anxiety. It is worth highlighting that focusing on negative stories in the media and via the internet is purposeful; human beings are designed to pay attention to risks and dangers. We will explore this in detail in the next chapter, but for now just remember that if the news is a potential trigger for anxiety and stress you should turn on some instrumental music instead. Identifying triggers is also an opportunity for you to model that behaviour to your children, but you need to know what sends your mind into a stress response before you can mitigate or eliminate such responses.

Knowing your triggers might mean you need to make a plan or come up with strategies for managing specific situations. If driving at night or on the highway makes your heart race for fear of being in an accident, then you may need to do some forward planning to either avoid or conquer such thoughts. This may require help from others, and so you need to be ready to organise that.

Not all triggers may relate to potentially dangerous situations. Some children do not like going to bed, for example, and you may find that helping your child go to bed at a reasonable hour creates anxiety. Maybe you need to come up with a plan that includes rewarding your child in some way to stop them from protesting. Remember that you don't want to put the responsibility on your child to manage your stress. Instead, we want you to be grounded and proactive in devising ways to manage your tolerance to various stressors. Again, there are teachable moments for your children when you implement a plan to curb specific anxious moments and demonstrate that stress can be managed and tolerated.

Teachable moments are an important part of parenting. When you learn strategies for managing anxiety and stress that work for you, then you can also pass them on to your children. For example, when they are stressed, teaching your children to think as rationally as possible, given their age, can be modelled and discussed. Saying that you understand they are scared but talking through the unlikelihood of something scary actually happening is easily doable. We do this when children have bad dreams, and we can also do this when life throws up some unexpected challenges. Remember too that your actions can impact your child even if you are not aware of it.

The late and world-renowned psychologist Professor Albert Bandura taught us a great deal about how children pick up on adult behaviours and actions and model them or literally make them part of who they are. Social learning theory – or more colloquially, "children see, children do" – tells us that our children are keen observers who can learn to mimic how we act and react. They observe your facial cues and expressions, the words you use and the emotions you display, and their sponge-like brains pick up everything you might show them. If you can display a calm, neutral and rational disposition when things go awry, then your children will learn to do so as well.

Modelling stress tolerance is very critical for children to observe. And while you may not want your child to see every anxious moment you experience, we would not want you to suppress your emotions. Instead, find an opportunity to explain why you may have acted the way you did. This might mean a conversation about how a recent event seemed to frustrate you and how, after reflection, you might have handled the situation differently. When anxiety and stress engage our fight-or-flight responses, it is unlikely we will always be at our best. However, when things calm down we are better placed to consider and talk about what we said or did, or what we might say or do in the future, and find a better way forward; again, a teachable moment.

Finally, be sure to be kind to yourself. As parents, we often second guess what we do, and that is only natural. However, to communicate any sense of calm to a child becomes very difficult when a parent is struggling with their own anxiety, and constantly questioning yourself or the world around you can unwittingly convey a sense of anxiety. Try to stay calm and focus on the positives. This is one of the foundational tenets underpinning this book. Parents need to stay grounded – grounded in their own health and well-being, physically and mentally, and grounded in the reality that life itself is far better now than in any other generation. The goal is not only to alleviate anxiety and stress but also to build resilience. Showing resilience in how you approach life in general rubs off on children. Always remember that life is good, in spite of what may be conveyed via the media and various other sources.

The next chapter offers some reasons for optimism and positivity when the world may appear to suggest otherwise.

Ground Rules

1. Anxiety, stress and trauma are related but are not the same thing. It is important to know the differences.

2. Not all stress leads to trauma. Positive stress or "eustress" is adaptive and can build resilience and confidence. Tolerable stress can be overcome with time and support while toxic stress may require stronger interventions.

3. Schools and teachers are in a position to support children and parents, but should not be relied upon for any measure of therapy.

4. You are the best person to help your children build resilience and adaptive mechanisms to buffer anxiety and stress.

5. How you act and react when life challenges you will teach your children how they might respond in similar situations. Be mindful of taking care of yourself and modelling positive approaches to anxiety and stress.

Five

Know Thy Child's School Well

> "There are many who believe therapism in the schools is a benign, constructive influence that comforts children, calming their fears and enhancing their feelings of self-acceptance. The evidence, however, does not bear this out."
>
> – Christina Hoff Sommers and Dr Sally Satel[25]

When Schools Become a Problem

In the last chapter we spent a bit of time looking at how schools often play a part in supporting children who have experienced stress, anxiety and/or trauma. We acknowledged that schools and teachers can be helpful in providing safe and supportive environments. We also briefly noted that school environments can contribute to anxiety, stress and even trauma. And finally, we cautioned against those teachers who, while acting in the place of parents or *in loco parentis*, also take on a persona akin to being a therapist. In this chapter we want to expand on these themes to give you a sense of how to keep yourself and your children grounded when schools become a problem and not part of a solution.

First, let us begin by saying that we are not trying to suggest that teachers would explicitly set out to harm students. We are ourselves educators and we train future educators. Every semester we are greeted by so many students who are keen to make a difference in the lives of children and teenagers alike as future teachers. And while some might jokingly say they want to teach for the time off in summer, none say they are in it for the money. And without hesitation, all say that they love children or have a passion for helping students learn, thrive and grow into happy human beings. Our concerns lie with various ideas and approaches as to what constitutes "good" education along with those who, despite having the best interests of children at heart, overstep their professional expertise. Let's start with schools and some of the things that we know can, and often do, contribute to anxiety and stress.

The first thing to explore was noted in the previous chapter and relates to pushing students to do things too soon. Increasingly we see this in the early years, where the last couple of decades have seen an academic curriculum being thrust towards younger and younger children. Throughout Australia, the first formal year of "schooling" usually occurs when children are four years old. Some states call this "kindergarten", while others refer to "pre-primary", "reception", "transition" and "preparatory" (or "prep", as it is more colloquially known). Whatever the label, there can be a great deal of stress for some children at this time, depending on the approach used to engage young students in learning. We will use prep in Queensland as an example.

The history of preschool in Queensland goes back to 1875, with numerous recommendations being made about the appropriate age for starting school (with various labels). More recently, prep was introduced in 2007 but became compulsory a decade later. Today prep is part of the P-3 curriculum – that is, prep to year three – which is typically designated as the "early years" of learning. Most children who enter prep are four years old. Those are the basics, but allow us to peruse a few problematic assumptions and some misguided notions of teaching young children.

First, it is worth noting that no two children are the same, so the following points are made in relation to what we know, and what the research tells us, to be most beneficial for children in the early years, especially in prep.

Many believe that when a child arrives for compulsory schooling for the first time they need to be able to do certain things, such as recite the alphabet, count to 100, or write their name, or to have other school-"readiness" skills. The truth is: children need good social skills and good oral language skills. If your child gets along well with others and likes to talk and have conversations, then they are already on the road to success. And that road to success is paved with play!

Play-based Learning

The first year of schooling should be all about what is referred to as "play-based" learning. The importance of play is evident in all mammals, and human beings are no exception. Play is an essential contributor to wiring a child's brain towards becoming a functioning adult. Play-based learning has an extensive array of empirical evidence telling us that this is the best framework for children in prep. For some, this approach should go beyond prep and be the basis of all early learning endeavours. Now, we could go on and on about the benefits, merits and validity of a play-based curriculum, but you can find the evidence yourself with a simple google search.[26] Instead, we'd like to highlight what can happen when you ask children to engage in an academic type of curriculum in the place of one based on play.

Let's start with some easy and common-sense truths. At age four, most children, particularly boys, are not ready for sitting at desks and doing "school". Anyone with a son can tell you that sitting still and paying attention to something is not an easy proposition for him. All children, but especially boys, are designed to move. Keep in mind, also, that on most measures, including oral language, boys lag behind girls, sometimes by as much as 18 to 24 months.

It is not uncommon for a three-year-old girl to have a greater gift of the gab than her older brother, and this advantage is all about developmental timelines.

The oral language difference between boys and girls is one of the reasons why the formal teaching of literacy does not happen in many countries prior to age seven, when those differences even out. In Finland, a country that routinely tops the charts in literacy and numeracy globally, the early years are all about relationships, play, adventure, exploration, curiosity and doing things young children are developmentally ready to do. Yet in Australia we expect children to start learning to read and write as soon as possible. What might that encourage? Here is some food for thought.

In 2013 the Queensland Government started to move away from a play-based curriculum in prep to a more academic style of teaching. No, it wasn't about having kids sit all day and practise writing or doing things with numbers per se – although some early childhood educators we know left the profession because that was what was happening – but it did involve less time learning by playing with well-designed activities in well-designed spaces. After all, prep was all about preparing children for year one, so best get them doing things five- and six-year-olds might be doing.

What might an outcome of such a switch be? From 2013 to 2019, across the state of Queensland, school suspensions of four-year-olds – allow us to repeat that for emphasis: *four-year-olds* – more than tripled! Was Queensland suddenly immersed in a generation of deviance, or was something else afoot? We are going to take a bit of liberty and speculate, as it would be very difficult to prove what we are about to say.

Imagine a four-year-old boy being asked to sit at a desk for a period of time. Not easy! Then that same boy is asked to hold a pencil and copy his name from a worksheet; he is being asked to use a writing instrument for which he lacks the manual dexterity or coordination for any measure of proficiency. Again, not easy! After some time, this boy gets frustrated and has had enough. What he is unlikely to do is raise his hand, express his frustrations cogently and eloquently, and ask for time out from the task. Instead, he may try to push another student to failure, and/or annoy those around him, and/or have a tantrum and start down a path of throwing things around the room, creating a hazard to others. If that is the case, then he will soon be going home.

This is not to suggest that there aren't any problematic children in schools, but how could suspensions for four-year-olds jump from roughly 500 to more than 1500 in six years?

The example is real. And although we speculate with regards to cause, as noted, one thing is undeniable. Trying to get children to do things they are not developmentally ready for can create frustrations, anger, anxiety and stress. Early learning environments that are structured and sedentary can produce negative effects on creativity as well as on social and emotional development and overall well-being.

There are other things that happen in schools that can create anxiety and stress for many children. Homework and high-stakes testing are two examples. It is beyond the scope or intent of this book to map out the arguments against many aspects of homework and testing, especially standardised testing. Both practices are deeply embedded in the culture of education in Australia and are not easily changed, in spite of the research suggesting we should do so. Instead, let us return to Finland for some comparative food for thought.[27]

In Finland, teachers do not believe that homework necessarily leads to better learning or better outcomes, and students rarely get more than a half-hour of homework per day. In fact, most students can complete most of any homework they might have before leaving for home. In Australia, however, homework is often lauded as a necessary evil of learning, and the older you get, the more the better. Trying to measure the impact of homework is not easy, and as such opinions on this topic vary, as they do when it comes to testing.

Testing of sorts does happen in Finland. However, standardised testing, like NAPLAN in Australia, is simply not done in Finland, and indeed in many other countries. And this is for good reason. The evidence around the efficacy of standardised testing shows that it lowers standards. So, while opinions may vary, time and time again the research evidence tells us that high-stakes testing like that in standardised tests does more harm than good.

As researchers, academics and authors, we are well aware that the views on homework and testing presented here may be controversial. We only ask you, as a parent, to consider that, while it is exceedingly difficult to find any empirical evidence of the benefits of homework and testing, one very demonstrable and common outcome is anxiety and stress. This means that you will be an important buffer to your children if such anxiety arises. It is also noteworthy that in Finland, where homework is rare and testing is infrequent and rarely high stakes, academic outcomes are among the world's best, and Finnish students experience less anxiety and stress in school than their peers in many other countries. Surely that is something to strive for: learning environments with less stress and better outcomes for all.

While it might be very difficult to change the status of homework and testing in your child's school, it is still a good idea to remain grounded and connected to what is going on there. If your child is coming home from school frustrated, anxious or stressed, then it would be a good idea to get to the bottom of what's going on. After all, school should not become a place where learning dives while stress thrives. Nor should it be a place where a teacher routinely becomes something more than their job description allows.

Teachers as Activists

By now, it is probably apparent that much of our message in this book focuses on the interacting and intricately interconnected heart–brain–body development of our kids and how we might ensure that the environments in which they grow and learn are supportive of their most optimal and robust development. It should also be clear that we place parents at the forefront of support not only for their children but also for themselves. Being grounded in all you do allows you to nurture yourself and by association your children. Being grounded also means you are acutely aware of any factors that might contribute to anxiety or stress in yourself or your children, lest those factors become traumatic. This includes what happens between your child and their teacher.

As educators who have worked collectively on five continents across a number of countries and many years, we have witnessed a couple of worrying cultural transitions in western schools. Increasingly, classrooms have become places where teachers espouse activist positions and/or offer therapeutic interventions. It is our contention that – however well-meaning teachers may be, and whatever good intentions they may have – there are some things that are not part of the art and science of teaching. And to be clear, activism and therapeutic interventions have never been part of any teacher training we have seen or been involved in. Allow us to explore each. We will start with a story about activism gone wrong.

Years ago, while doing research in a primary school, Michael came across a relatively new year seven teacher who felt it important to expand on the science curriculum and have her students consider how cattle might be contributing to climate change. In itself, climate change was only a very small and tangential part of the curriculum, but this teacher's vegetarian and social justice leanings meant she had a personal stake in changing the minds of the young people around her.

Over the course of two or three weeks, students were presented with information about the "plight" of the planet and global warming at the intersection of beef consumption and cattle raising. They were taught something that is still in the public zeitgeist: cows fart and this is a major contributor to greenhouse gases. Therefore, she suggested, the students would all do well to eat less beef and spread the word – hamburgers are bad for the planet. Insert gasps of disbelief, if you wish, but such adventures in political minefields are not terribly rare in schools. Unfortunately for this teacher, she found out quickly how things can go wrong when teaching merges into activism.

Parents of one of her students contacted the principal to arrange a meeting, which in fact became a dressing down of that teacher. You see, these parents were the proud franchise owners of not one, but three burger joints! They had made a very good living and provided for their children every time someone stepped through the doors of their three golden-arched establishments.

Now you may see some humour in this, but the seriousness of the issue should not be underestimated. A teacher felt the need to extend her beliefs into her classroom. No doubt she thought her intentions were noble and just. However, discussion of political, social and cultural issues should always be left for parents, who are entitled to educate their children as they see fit. Education is meant to provide students with the essential skills for them to succeed in life. And while we would agree that these go beyond reading, writing and arithmetic, any look at the trials and tribulations of our time must embody opportunities to examine a diversity of views and weigh up conflicting viewpoints and arguments in a rational, objective way. More importantly, such topics must be explored with the consent of the parents and not at the whim of someone's personal beliefs or ideologies.

Now, we are not here to suggest that teachers cannot be vegetarians or have political agendas; only that any attempts to explore controversial topics should only be made if they are part of the curriculum and explored in a non-partisan fashion. Discussion with evidence is one thing; activism is completely different. In the current social and cultural milieu of our society, teachers should not become arbiters of political hot potatoes, especially those that may not align with parents' views or, more worryingly, might instil anxiety or fear. Climate change, for example, is a highly political and contentious issue often wrapped in doomsday scenarios and hyperbole that can stress adults, never mind children. Teachers should therefore proceed with caution; and you, as a parent, have every right to ensure your child is grounded in a positive atmosphere and not being taught – or dare we say, indoctrinated –with fear. The world is not as scary as many might suggest, nor is it on the verge of some global catastrophe, as claimed in some news, social media and information sources.

We explore this in more detail in Chapter 7. For now, we would just like to reiterate that knowing what is being taught to your children is very important, and when it deviates from the curriculum you need to have a say in the matter. Moreover, when something comes up in class causing anxiety and stress and requiring help, support and comfort, there are limits to what teachers can and should do.

Teachers as Therapists

It goes without saying that schools are places where mental health work happens, and teachers do have a role in supporting student mental health. They are trained to do this by learning how to create safe and supportive environments for learning. Within this framework, teachers learn to build positive relationships and promote healthy interactions with peers. They also learn how to adjust their craft to meet the learning needs of their students and provide opportunities for all to succeed and/or learn from their mistakes and failings. This is arguably the core business of teaching. In the last couple of decades, however, schools have become places for mediating many aspects of mental health and trauma, and teachers are adopting or being coached into adopting a more therapeutic professional persona.

Again, we want to emphasise that teachers do play a role in promoting and supporting mental health, and that that is an important job. This has become even more apparent since the pandemic, when those students who were locked out of school the longest had the highest incidences of poor mental health. It turns out that closing educational institutions at all levels weakened some of the very things that help maintain good mental health.[28] Lockdowns helped to create meltdowns because daily routines, social interactions and the support of teachers help buffer against poor mental health outcomes. In other words, schools, by their very nature, act as buffers against adverse events and experiences that might contribute to a student's anxiety, stress or trauma. This is an important component of "schooling", but it is also important to keep in mind that teachers are not therapists.

To reiterate, being safe and supportive is part and parcel of schooling. Human beings and relationships can be challenging, but schools offer a space to alleviate anxiety and stress. However, the extent to which schools and teachers can help support traumatised students in particular is questionable, depending on the nature of the trauma.

As discussed earlier in this book, we know that trauma can impact on all aspects of development and by association behaviour and school performance. We also know that there are genuinely traumatised children who come from backgrounds where war, famine, abuse and violence have played an integral part in who they are and who they will become. But we would contend that in such extreme situations, sometimes referred to as complex trauma, it is not within the scope of an educator's profession and skill set to "fix" or "heal" the trauma. Rather, the best that teachers can strive to do is be supportive and understanding of all children and bear in mind that when there are big reactions to small things a child's stress response system may be in overdrive. By its nature, trauma is an overactive stress response, but there are very simple, grounded ways in which parents and teachers can work to support children without going into deep psychology and the professional arenas of qualified mental health practitioners. You should leave the complex trauma to the experts, but parents and teachers can make a difference.

Parents can work to create low-stress environments. They can build self-awareness and ensure that, to the best of their ability, they do not overreact to situations and move anxiety to stress or even to trauma. Without rationalising and without further stressing children who are struggling, parents can create supportive, loving environments, even if they don't solve the immediate problem. Throughout this book, we have provided strategies for parents to mitigate their own stress and by association that of the home environment.

Teachers, on the other hand, must recognise and understand that all behaviour is a response to students' environments and environmental stresses. Students who are anxious, stressed or traumatised may find learning difficult and may display challenging behaviours such as swearing, being disrespectful, or being a bully, while also displaying poor emotional regulation with low resilience. Knowing that behaviours are symptomatic of other issues reminds teachers to find ways to navigate those challenges calmly and in a way that is supportive and measured. Such an approach also replaces the risks of exacerbating behaviour issues through punishment or pathologising a child with a more restorative model. This underpins much of our philosophy in this book and helps sum up this chapter.

It is important to understand that no one escapes the damaging things that happen in the world completely, and we all experience anxiety, stress and sometimes trauma. Perhaps moving away from any idea that some people are absolutely fine while others are traumatised would help to create a more compassionate, less pathologised view of human beings and in particular children. We believe that, barring any measure of disorder, such compassion comes naturally to parents.

We also believe that parents should be aware of all that goes on in the school environs. Well-meaning teachers may not always act in the best interests of a child. Teachers are generally compassionate, supportive and caring, but compassion should not extend beyond the scope of their role as an educator. Teachers and parents alike may sometimes need help, and we would encourage them to seek this when necessary. Supporting children regardless of what they have been through requires sensitivity. Teachers in particular should not put the burden of "fixing" trauma on themselves, despite their best intentions, nor should they amplify anxiety, stress or trauma with their particular views about the world around them. Overcoming anxiety, stress and trauma is mainly about building resilience, and we discuss this in more detail in the next couple of chapters. For now, we close with a reminder that helping children thrive in the world, with all of its problems and complexities, requires a community approach, but the head of that community is the parent.

Ground Rules

1. Know your child's school and what they are being taught. Have regular discussions about what they are doing and learning. If your child comes home showing signs of distress, it is time to ask questions.

2. Watch for signs of anxiety or stress arising from frustration. Young children in particular can demonstrate challenging behaviours when they feel they are unable to do what is asked of them.

3. Watch out for the creeping of activism into the curriculum. However well-intentioned teachers might be, you are the person who discusses contentious issues and problems with your child.

4. Be wary of any attempts to pathologise your child's behaviour. Behaviour should be monitored and discussed collectively, and if your child is struggling, then a deep dive into why that is occurring is important.

5. At all times keep communication channels open and thriving with your child. It is important to know what is happening at school and in the wider environment.

Building Resilience in the Real World

> "Teens who spend more time with their friends in person are happier, less lonely, and less depressed while those who spend more time on social media are less happy, lonelier and more depressed... online time does not protect against loneliness and depression, while in-person time does."
>
> – Professor Jean M. Twenge[29]

The Downside of Technology in the Classroom

From 2000 to 2019 BC (Before Covid), the world was changing very rapidly for young and old alike. In Chapter 3 we mentioned how advances in technology and increasing access to screen devices were having a net negative effect on young people. In this chapter we want to expand on that topic. We also want to look at how media, social and otherwise, along with other sources of information, such as the internet, are fostering environments of fear, stress and anxiety.

Some of you might find some of our ideas contestable, and we welcome the debate of ideas. In the end, we ask you, the reader, to consider the following pages with an open mind and heart so that you can create an environment that builds resilience over anxiety, strength over fear and optimism over pessimism. It is our contention that a mind wrapped in a healthy mental disposition free of anxiety and stress is the best "safe" space for young people when it comes to conquering adversity. It is also the best version of you for helping your children to thrive.

To begin this chapter, which focuses on screen devices and social media, we'd like to start with a proclamation: we are not Luddites or what some might call Neo-Luddites these days. We question the omnipotence of technology in the lives of young people, not with a view to rejecting technology outright but rather in our understanding of what constitutes healthy development and what hinders that development. There is no stopping the runaway technology train. Screens are now firmly situated in the lives of people of all ages. However, the ever-expanding array of technology available to the masses is being mirrored by equally expanding volumes of research telling us that screen time is a problem for all and especially for those whose brains are still developing.

Yes, technology continues to expand its reach. As adults, however, we can make adjustments in our lives when it comes to how much or how little time we spend on screen devices. Arguably, this may be difficult for a new generation of adults known as "Gen Z" who have grown up with screens and whose hands often seem glued to their phones. Children and teens are a different story, however, and do require guidance, support and modelling. That is your job, and we will refer to that throughout this chapter, but first we want to focus on the young brains and minds around us.

When looking at the potential problems of screens for young people, it is important to remember our earlier discussions and most notably that the human brain does not fully mature until the mid-twenties. It is also important to remember that the brain is literally shaped by our experiences, and young brains are very impressionable. Relatedly, from birth to age four the brain is busy mapping out its neuro-superhighways of connectivity, and then later during the teen years it is busy restructuring itself. During all of our developing years, but most notably in those just noted, the brain is soaking up information that helps to shape who we are and what we will become. Therefore, and even before looking at any evidence, it should be obvious that what children see and do can shape who they are and will be. Prior to the beginning of this century, and apart from television, movies and some video games, most of the experiences children were exposed to were in the "real" world and not dominated by computers. So, let's look back a bit and explore what has changed and where we are now.

The use of personal computers in homes and at work began to take hold from the mid-1980s. The internet became readily available to the public in the early 1990s and email came along not long after. By 1999 things were really beginning to change rapidly in terms of the presence of computers in the everyday lives of most people. As the year 2000 approached, much of the world held its collective breath as something called Y2K was about to unleash untold havoc on humanity with the arrival of the new millennium. Some thought that all computers on the planet would crash, planes would fall out of the skies, and all manner of telecommunications would become hindered by devices that could not handle the switch from 1999 to 2000. Fortunately, all the doomsday prophesies fell flat. The world was safe, computers kept on ticking along, and technology continued advancing with the world wide web, "wifi" and increasingly smaller computers becoming commonplace. In 2007 the first widely available "smartphone" hit the markets. Social media emerged not long afterwards, and the world has never looked back.

Computers – in the shape of tablets, laptops and most commonly smartphones – are everywhere. Today, conservative estimates suggest that more than 95 percent of western children can competently use a mobile device by age 4, most by age 1. No more than a generation ago, toddlers weren't even exposed to computers, and now they hold them, the world and a myriad of content in the palm of their hands.

Proponents of children using technology abound with a variety of arguments for ongoing and increased use at home and in schools. Suggestions that computers are a "must-have" panacea for learning, or that children will somehow be left behind if they don't use screen devices, are commonplace. Interestingly, there isn't any evidence to support such claims, with some studies saying just the opposite. The Organisation for Economic and Co-operative Development (OECD) offers a good example.

In 2015 the OECD published a report noting that the use of computers in schools and the associated costs of investments in technology infrastructure were not paying off. They noted that countries that used technology and the internet the most were performing more poorly on international tests in mathematics, literacy and science than those that used technology the least. In fact, Andreas Schleicher, the Head of Education at the OECD, stated that "the reality is that technology is doing more harm than good in our schools today".[30] Now, you may be wondering why we would note the OECD's perspective on technology in schools. Well, this is the same organisation that the federal government looks to every three years to see how Australian students are doing in comparison to their peers around the globe via something known as PISA.

PISA is an acronym for the Programme for International Student Assessment. Every three years the OECD launches a worldwide testing program to evaluate educational systems by measuring 15-year-old students' scholastic performance in mathematics, science and reading. The testing started in 2000, and Australian students have dropped in the rankings ever since; as of the last testing, Australian students dropped from 6th to 25th in mathematics, 8th to 14th in science, and 4th to 16th in reading. These results have been turned into political hot potatoes every three years by politicians who blame their opponents and declare the need for raising standards. We've never come across an argument for lowering standards, so we will give them some credit for their proclamations. However, what the politicians never discuss, or conveniently omit, is the fact that Australian schools, according to the OECD's report on computers and schooling noted earlier, lead the world in their use of the internet and technology. Now remember, Australian results have dropped every PISA reporting period. Hmm, might there be a connection between poor outcomes and screen time?

It is difficult to establish a causal link between screen time and poor academic outcomes per se, but we've yet to come across any scientific evidence showing that technology enhances test scores, grades or outcomes in any demonstrable way. Government reports with shiny covers showing kids using iPads with pages full of platitudes about the need for screen devices abound, but with little or no empirical evidence to support such assertions. Computers are tools, nothing more, and should not be held up as the key to your child's success in a classroom. If a school administrator, principal or teacher tells you otherwise, ask for the evidence.

Now, we're confident that the preceding few paragraphs will ruffle the feathers of many IT gurus, academics and bureaucrats, but it is up to them to show us the long-term benefits of screen time within the research literature. After all, we believe that anything we do to, and with, children should be based on the best available evidence. This is especially true given the cost of resourcing technology, the challenges with managing it in a classroom, and its capacity for adding to the overall daily time children spend on screens. It's also important to keep in mind that if other places around the world, according to the OECD, are doing fine with less technology, then any argument for its use must be persuasive and backed by evidence.

Screen Time as a Public Health Issue

Issues around students, screens and schools are one thing. More problematic is our contention that screen time must now be considered a major public health issue and that reducing screen time must become the new priority for child and adolescent health and well-being. We feel this is especially significant if we are talking about alleviating stress and anxiety and building resilience. Allow us to explain!

We have been writing about children, teens and screen use for many years and have conducted and compiled numerous studies telling us that screen time is highly problematic for young developing minds. When computers were first being introduced into schools, there wasn't a great deal of concern or push-back, as most of the time they were simply another resource to be used, installed in computer labs and guided by teachers.

Over a very short period, computers morphed into handheld devices that could do more than simple word processing or research. With these changes came "apps" with access to social media, games, gambling and pornography with the simple touch of a button. Over time, we have come to learn that screen time and its associated applications are highly problematic for children and teens.

In the early days of research on screen use, studies often focused on the impact of video games, and in particular violent video games, on immature brains. A major concern was whether playing violent video games would make a person more violent or not. Much of this stemmed from the many horrific mass school shootings in the United States, where people were looking for motives behind such heinous crimes. As it turns out, a common denominator of all who have perpetrated the horrendous and inexplicable act of gunning down children and adults in schools is that they have indeed spent a great deal of time playing violent video games, especially first-person shooter games, as they are known. And while research around this topic is very contentious, there isn't any strong evidence to suggest that violent games alone would make someone violent or commit a mass shooting. There are simply too many other variables that contribute to the making of a mass murderer; it could be that those with mental health issues who are prone to violence simply like to play violent games. However, there is ample evidence to suggest that violent games may indeed make young people more aggressive or desensitise them to violent behaviour. Although this is worrisome, it is somewhat tangential to our fundamental concerns regarding screen use, and anyone interested in the connections between video games and aggression can find a great deal of information on this topic elsewhere.[31] We are more interested in the growing body of research findings indicating an association between screen time and adverse physical and mental health conditions. Let's start with a few important facts before looking at some research.

First, the developing brain, as discussed in detail in earlier chapters, is literally shaped by experience. This means that all aspects of your child's mind, including thinking, attitudes, emotions and behaviour, are influenced by what happens in the environment. The famed child psychologist Haim Ginott captures this beautifully when he states: "Children are like wet cement. Whatever falls on them makes an impression".[32]

Second, while we live in a futuristic digital world compared to previous generations, our developmental, psychological, emotional and social needs are still very much part of our prehistoric DNA. The human brain has evolved over time and has been fine-tuned through thousands of years of experiences that did not involve swiping up or down, push notifications, "influencers" or curating friends in a virtual world. Over the last couple of decades, our brains have been bombarded with information in a way that would have been unfathomable even a generation ago. This means that the experiences needed for healthy development are being hijacked by "big tech". We are only just beginning to understand this in any detail.

Finally, and before noting some major emerging issues associated with screen use and young minds, let us be clear on one very important matter. Those who design the devices, the apps, and all the bells and whistles that come with the divine glow of a screen, are not in it to make the world a better place. Sure, we concede that warm and fuzzy comments about helping children learn and grow, or creating more equitable environments, can be found in the mission statements of many tech and media companies. But at the end of the day, the goal is to make money, and to make money you need people to use your product, and if you can hook them early then you have potential lifelong customers. This was the business model of big tobacco companies in the 1950s and it's now being emulated by big tech companies. Yes, you may be thinking this all sounds a bit hyperbolic or cynical, but let us shed some light on why we make such claims.

The Perils of Living Virtually

Since the year 2000 there has been an exponential growth in research focusing on children, teens, screen time, smartphone use and all manner of applications that can now be used in the palm of our hands. Unsurprisingly, this has corresponded with the pervasive availability and use of technology and screen devices. Advances in technology have provided us with greater medical and scientific insights into the brain, its neuroarchitecture, how it works, and how the environment might be impacting on its development. Advances in medical and psychological research have also helped to fill in some gaps in terms of understanding how screens might impact on our bodies and minds. Here are just a few things we have learned over the last couple of decades about the downside of technology that come with a fair degree of authority and a great deal of evidence.

Perhaps the most obvious negative impact associated with screen devices is an increase in sedentary behaviour. You may have heard the phrase "sitting is the new smoking", and there is ample evidence to support this.

Earlier we referred to the brain as still being prehistoric in how it functions and develops over time. One other thing that is historically ingrained in our brains and our genetic design is the fact that human beings are not meant to be sedentary, isolated and glued to a screen. The value of exercise and physical activity to overall physical and mental health is well documented. We feel better physically and mentally when we are active; so much so that physical activity is not just good for the body but is a known buffer for preventing and healing depression. Yet, we have become increasingly sedentary. It appears that that the pandemic exacerbated sedentary behaviour as people were told to stay indoors, work or learn from home on a screen, and curtail physical activity beyond their own yard. Is it coincidence that during and after the pandemic rates of depression tripled in those areas where people were locked down and prescribed screens for engaging in relationships, work and life? We think not, and the evidence seems to say as much. We need to move, and children need to move more, to ensure all aspects of healthy development.

As well as promoting sedentary behaviour, screens are also impacting on how we rest and rejuvenate our bodies and minds. The literature on the effects of screens on sleep is extensive and refers to a particular type of light.

There are many types and colours of light, but not all of these impact us in the same way. Blue light is a good example, and like other colours of visible light, it is all around us; the sun emits blue light. Blue light is helpful and beneficial during daylight hours because it boosts attention, reaction times and mood. When night falls, however, blue light can be problematic, even though natural blue light is retreating as the sun goes down.

When the sun starts to set and we feel sleepy, that is because melatonin is working its magic. Melatonin is a neurotransmitter that induces sleep, and while light of any kind can suppress the secretion of melatonin, blue light at night does so more powerfully. And guess what emits a great deal of blue light? If you said screen devices, you'd be correct. Being on a screen increases exposure to blue light, and blue light, in turn, keeps us awake! Researchers have even identified that blue light suppresses melatonin for about twice as long as other light and shifts our sleep cycles by as much as three hours.[33] In other words, if you would naturally feel sleepy around nine in the evening, being on a screen might suppress that feeling until midnight. This is also true for your children and especially problematic for teens.

During the teen years adolescent sleep cycles can shift by as much as two to three hours. As if puberty wasn't rough enough! Remember when your eight-year-old might have been sleepy by eight at night?

For a teenager, that sense of sleepiness and subsequent bedtime is now likely to be past your bedtime. We know that teenagers need about nine hours of sleep a night, and most are not getting anywhere near that for any number of reasons. However, if your teenager is on a screen late at night, then that lack of sleep is exacerbated. When your child needs to get up the next morning for school, it could look like an audition for *The Walking Dead*! Your job is to get them off screens early and model that behaviour yourself, but this becomes ever more challenging when the screen devices we use have a now not-so-hidden agenda.

Perhaps the most redeeming feature of modern-day screen devices and their apps is that they are designed to be user friendly. On the dark side, however, they are also designed to be user addictive.

Researchers have a pretty good understanding of the mechanics of addiction, which starts with the feel-good neurotransmitter dopamine and how it works in the brain's reward system. When you engage in behaviours that elevate dopamine, you feel good, which in turn makes you want to repeat whatever you were doing so you can maintain those pleasurable feelings. This can create a feedback loop of wanting the pleasurable reward again, and again, and again. Eating chocolate can elevate dopamine 50 percent, having sex 100 percent, and nicotine 150 percent, while illicit drugs such as cocaine can ramp up dopamine 225 percent and crystal meth a staggering 1000 percent.[34]

You may be thinking that if there is a constant loop of dopamine desire then wouldn't we all just be doing more of the same all the time to get that "feel good" feeling? Well, we also have something that helps put the brakes on things: our frontal lobes. These important parts of our brain allow us to think through the consequences of what we do and make responsible decisions, or what you might simply call "if… then" thinking. Remember too that this part of the brain doesn't fully mature until we are in our mid-twenties.

You may also be wondering what dopamine and addiction have to do with screen devices and social media. Well, consider that in 2017

Sean Parker, Facebook's first president, publicly admitted that the company he had helped Mark Zuckerberg establish had designed its platform with algorithms that were intended to help spike dopamine and get people hooked on it. For example, features such as the "like" button give users a little dopamine hit and encourage them to upload and view more content. We all like to be liked!

Not to be outdone, Tristan Harris, former Google product manager, made headlines the same year by telling the public that Silicon Valley had been in the business of engineering apps, smartphones, and other devices to *get people hooked*, because the more an individual used these platforms and devices, the more money the developers made. He even noted that some programmers called such initiatives "brain hacking" – programmed methods of hijacking people's minds to form a habit. In Silicon Valley, the home of Google, Facebook and other big tech companies, design techniques are embedded inside the products to make smartphones so appealing that people use them, and other devices, more often.

In 2017 both Parker and Harris felt morally obliged to let the public know that screens, apps and social media have a goal, and that goal is to hook a person into using them as much as possible. The world now has a full complement of digital drugs that didn't exist before. Ominously, Parker in characterising the Facebook business model, went so far as to state to reporters: "God only knows what it's doing to our children's brains."[35] God only knows indeed! Actually, we mortals know some things as well.

Risky Business

As alluded to earlier, it is well known that there are inherent risks related to addiction and screen use. For example, we now know that certain smartphone apps and video games can pump up dopamine 100 percent. Think about that: screens can be as pleasurable to the brain as having sex! We also know that chronic exposure to addictive substances or behaviours reduces the grey matter in the prefrontal lobes, the brain's CEO. This is the brain's decision-making centre or braking system, as noted earlier, and addictive behaviours such as prolonged time on screens appears to be able to break the brakes! And finally, we know that a young person's brain is likely more vulnerable to things going wrong, given its plastic nature and the fact that it is not yet fully developed.

Sedentary behaviour, sleep disruption and addiction are three potentially harmful ways in which screens can impact on our children's physical and mental health. Clinical and brain-imaging studies have also demonstrated links between screen time and usage with increases in depression, anxiety, ADHD and thoughts of self-harm.[36] Recently a very worrying phenomenon known as "virtual autism" has also been associated with screen time. To understand virtual autism it is important to have some sense of our current understanding of autism itself.

Autism is a pervasive neuro-developmental disorder or more precisely a neuro-connectivity disorder (some brain regions present too many or too few neural connections) with moderate genetic hereditability. Without getting too technical, autism is seen as a spectrum of disorders, which is referred to as Autistic Spectrum Disorder or ASD. On one end of the continuum, those with profound autism may be non-verbal or minimally verbal with a low IQ and present many challenges requiring help with the daily tasks of life. On the other end of that same continuum are university-bound students who have unusual talents or abilities but struggle with social and cultural mannerisms – think Sheldon Cooper of *Big Bang Theory* television fame.

Diagnosis of autism has risen from less than 1 per 1000 people in the 1960s to about 17 per 1000 today. Data from the United States Centres for Disease Control and Prevention (CDC) noted that the prevalence of ASD doubled between 2000 and 2018, with males outnumbering females by roughly four to one.[37] Trying to understand why there seems to be an increase in ASD is currently anyone's guess. Researchers and clinicians are looking to provide further insights into the condition itself and what might contribute to its increasing prevalence. One such clinician and an expert in ASD has shifted his gaze towards screens and young minds.

Marius Zamfir is a Romanian clinical psychologist who had anecdotally noticed that the incidence of autism increased very suddenly from the beginning of the century. In 2018 he introduced the term "virtual autism" to the world based on his clinical work with children. His was the first study to confirm this form of autism which has now been documented in several countries and is the subject of articles published in a variety of scientific journals.

At the core of Zamfir's work is his identification of a relationship between Intensive Early Screen Exposure (IESE) with a range of symptoms and behaviours that mimic or are consistent with ASD in children under six years of age. In a nutshell, Zamfir has observed the emergence of ASD-like behaviours in otherwise undiagnosed children when they have been on screens for more than four hours a day over extended periods of time.

Now, some might be very wary to suggest that screens are causing autism, but that is not what Zamfir and others suggest. What they are saying is that being on screens for extensive periods of time deprives a child of all of the things it needs for normal healthy development, especially for social and emotional development. Zamfir believes that there is a direct causal link between excessive consumption (over 4-5 hours per day) of a virtual environment (smartphone, tablet, TV, laptop, etc.) and ASD-specific behaviours.[38] Put simply, he thinks too much time on screens makes children behave like ASD children. Common sense tells us that time on screens deprives a child of time in the real world of human interactions which are critical for all aspects of healthy development.

Since Zamfir's work was published, other studies have demonstrated links between early-life screen exposure and ASD-like symptoms and ASD diagnoses. Some researchers have shown that children with a clinical diagnosis of ASD are also at risk of negative effects where screens exacerbate their existing behaviours. Some of the most recent brain-imaging research has also noted changes to regions of the brain associated with intensive screen use, with the reversal of these changes as something unknown.[39]

Now, we don't want you to beat yourself up if your children spend time on screens, but we do want you to consider the following. First, it should be apparent that too much time on screens is not a good thing. From the lack of physical activity to addiction to sleep disturbance to an array of mental health disorders, including the manifestation of ASD-like behaviours, screen time is indeed an issue for children and teens. Second, big tech is in the business of getting people hooked on their screens, so let's not forget the inherent risks associated with screen devices. Fortunately, and most importantly, all is not lost.

In working with parents in Romania whose children started to display ASD-like behaviours, Zamfir found that removing devices and getting children outdoors in the natural world for periods of two to three weeks' duration eliminated those behaviours. A digital detox is doable and may be necessary. And it seems that the outdoors is the place for this to happen. So, while the modern digital world can create a matrix of issues, Mother Nature appears to be a buffer and healer of all things done in binary code. The research around this is clear; being outdoors is good for us and especially so in the company of others.

In the end, what all of this means is that you, as a parent, must shift the balance from screens to trees and/or engagement with people in the real world when necessary. That is not too difficult or prescriptive, but of course this might mean you need to change your habits too! We can all be prone to losing ourselves in our screens, but as adults we can find a path out of a pixelated world into one that generations of humans have grown and thrived in. Interestingly, building resiliency happens in the real world. Once again, and regardless of the age of your children, you are the best role model for them. They need to see you switch off your device and spend time with them and others. This is the best recipe for helping build a healthy mind, especially in a world that is often portrayed as dangerous, as we shall see in the next chapter.

Ground Rules

1. The world has changed remarkably in the last couple of decades, but what the human brain needs for healthy development has not. Children and teens grow and thrive in "real" worlds where reciprocal relationships offer the best environment for that growth.

2. Screen devices should be considered as a potential threat to physical and mental health. They have been linked to a vast array of problems associated with their use.

3. The virtual world is not a place to build resiliency or relationships in. It cannot replicate all of the subtle things that occur when people engage with one another in real time and space.

4. As a parent, you need to avoid being lost in the matrix we call screen time and model the behaviour you'd like to see in your children. You may need to intervene and implement a digital detox and solicit Mother Nature's help as a buffer for this work. At the very least, you need to shift the balance from time on screens to time in the real world with real people.

Seven

Fear Not!

"Open the newspaper, watch the evening news. On any given day, there's a good chance that someone – a journalist, activist, consultant, corporate executive, or politician – is warning about an 'epidemic' of something or other that threatens you and those you hold dear... We are the healthiest, wealthiest, and longest-lived people in history. And we are increasingly afraid. This is one of the great paradoxes of our time."

– Daniel Gardner[40]

The World Is a Scary Place!

That's what the 24/7 news cycle would have you believe! But for our children, the immediate environment (home and school) is *their* world. And as parents, we are the creators of the most important immediate environment (home), so it's up to us whether the space our children grow in amplifies the "Bad Things Out There" – or not. It's as if the news cycle, regardless of where we look, would have us cowering in fear, terrified that our children will be abducted or kidnapped, or that they will face a tsunami brought about by imminent climate change, or that their future is bleak and there will be no animals left for them to love in the near future.

The worrying thing is: we should know better or at least know what is important to know about being fearful, because those who push fear upon us and our children certainly do. And what we know is this: the human brain is designed to be afraid in order to ensure our survival. Of all of our instincts and emotions, fear is the most powerful influence on our behaviour. Over many millennia, our brains have evolved to be alert for danger. Have you ever wondered why it is that you can travel anywhere in the world and people are likely to be wary of snakes? Being wary of snakes is literally hardwired into our brains – it's universal. Over thousands of years, human beings developed a healthy respect of snakes, among many other things. Those who didn't, well, chances are their family trees ended abruptly at some point!

So, we are fine-tuned to be on alert. Our brains are designed to survive and learn in that order, and fear helps us survive. We fight or flee depending on circumstances, and if you want to get someone's undivided attention, give them a dose of bad news, horrific events or apocalyptic proclamations and you will have them ready for action and looking for details. This is the business model for news channels and others who want your viewing attention.

But here's the thing: it is not in the best interests of our children to set their nervous systems on fire with existential fears about a world apparently on the brink of disaster. Regardless of what we believe, if we want our children to develop a healthy nervous system, where the sympathetic and parasympathetic branches are balanced, then we need to enable them to feel positive, empowered and grounded. We need to buffer them from those who would have them believe that danger lurks all around and the end is near.

Currently, one of the most prolific fear-inducing stories is that of the newly termed "global boiling". Though we won't go into it here, the jury is out on what is actually happening (for example, Antarctic ice has steadily expanded over the past 40 years, "confounding scientists" and is at an all-time high).[41] Instead of being whipped along by stories of the imminent extinction of everything we love, and passing that fear on to our children, we could take another approach that, in the end, is better for everyone. This approach will not induce a fight-or-flight response to the world. It will empower our children and enhance their lives. We need to support our kids so that they see the world as a beautiful place worth preserving and caring for. Pick up your litter; care for wild animals; don't waste water. These are things we can do as families out of love for our immediate and broader environment, not out of fear – and that will make all the difference. Our children are not mature enough to understand anything beyond *thinking locally and acting locally*. Even teens, whose brains are still developing and whose identities are still emerging and who struggle to do their homework and chores, are not in a good place for saving the world.

We also don't want our children to feel like terrible people who – if they aren't full of holy terror about their own imminent demise – will destroy the world with their carelessness. We don't want them to feel helpless in the face of everything bad that far more influential people may be doing. For the sakes of our children and ourselves, a far more powerful response to whatever is going on is to love our beautiful world and foster a love of the planet and our fellow humans, rather than fostering fear of one another and ourselves.

Our relationships with people, places and living things can be harmonious rather than fearful. We can choose to act out of love rather than fear. Fear engages the sympathetic nervous system, which sets off a cascade of "depleting" physiological processes that are necessary for short-term escape. Love and gratitude do the opposite and balance the autonomic nervous system, engaging "renewing" and repairing processes. So, regardless of our political beliefs and our ideologies, the reality is that if we focus on what we need to do to balance our own autonomic nervous systems and those of our children – we all win. What follows, then, are some grounded approaches that support family relationships and can help build a sense of self-worth in our children.

Fostering a "Growth Mindset"

Psychologist and author Carol Dweck has conducted numerous studies, and her research over decades has shown that if we acknowledge our children's efforts and endeavours – regardless of whether they win or lose – and admire their progress, they will not fear giving things a go. They will not feel stuck in narrow views of themselves, but be willing to try things even if they "fail". This is termed having a "growth mindset". Kids who have a growth mindset are ready to tackle challenges, to try things out, to risk falling – or not making it to the top – climbing the mountain for the sheer adventure of it, rather than for the goal of getting to the summit.[42]

So, what is a parent's role in this? If your kids are involved in sport or learning a musical instrument, encourage them. Appreciate progress. Admire their new skills. This will benefit them so much more than merely placing a value on winning gold somewhere. The journey is as important as the destination. And if they do win gold, awesome, but that wasn't the whole point. What did they learn along the way?

We can help our kids nurture their sense of self. We can look at the things that matter: their efforts in the world, how much they improve, what they learn, how they grow and change and acquire new strengths. And so we can show them that most failures are not really failures but unexpected outcomes that sometimes come with a gift of some new insight. We can still tell our kids they are wonderful humans, but we should beware of empty praise – of the "inverse power of praise" that Dweck talks about – and how that can play out as kids get fixed ideas of who they are and what they can achieve.

If we acknowledge our kids' successes in terms of how much ground they covered, rather than what trophies or awards they received, we allow them to breathe – to feel valid, regardless of whether they win or lose. If we don't get too fixated on the goal, our kids will be less likely to suffer in the narrow success/fail paradigm we too often live by.

Let's talk about family dynamics and the often fraught and frayed relationships that can develop between siblings or within the little societies that families are. There is one lens that can offer parents an approach to creating a peaceful home that will reduce stress and allow for warm and loving and honest family relationships. This is an investment over time. Results will be seen in weeks, months and years – not days.

As a facilitator in restorative practice, Shelley has worked with schools, communities, kids and families all over Australia to shift perspectives on the "ground rules" needed for establishing respectful, loving relationships in all settings. It is a low-stress approach and is not a substitute for consequences or even punishment. But it provides an opportunity for people to fix things between them before taking the punitive route.

The approach is different to the usual approach of punishment as the only consequence to a "crime". It teaches responsibility and accountability rather than shame and blame. It allows the person who is responsible for hurting someone to fix the harm.

The affective theory underpinning the restorative conversation has been tested over time and appears to offer one of the most powerful approaches we can take to make relationships in all spheres sustainable and capable of transformation.[43]

Importantly, it relies on people acknowledging the effect of their behaviour on others. It's a step offered before we say "Go to your room!" or "Now you're in time out!" – or whatever punitive measures parents may have in place.

The premise is that, in a restorative model, we define the wrong thing as *that which causes harm*. The wrong thing creates *responsibility and liability* on the part of the person who caused the harm. The other premise is that *everyone who is part of the problem is part of the solution.*

This engages everyone equally. There is no blame and no shame; only accountability and responsibility.

It works in the criminal justice system, and it has worked on a national level in many countries. New Zealand has had a restorative model in their youth justice system since 1989. South Africa's Truth and Reconciliation Commission lasted for years in the 1990s and allowed for deep healing, amnesty, consequences and reparations for those impacted by the crimes committed during the Apartheid era.

In the restorative model, we work first to identify who has been harmed and in what way. We then look at what needs to be done in order for this harm to be repaired. Whether it's a broken window, a stolen toy or hurt feelings, this approach can work for families, for siblings, as long as everyone is on board. The process is very simple and can be distilled into three important questions asked of every person involved:

- What happened?
- Who has been hurt and how?
- How do we fix things?

How would you introduce this approach to your family? You might start out by saying something at dinner like: "Hey guys, in this family from now on we're going to have this agreement: when something is broken, we fix it. Windows, toys, feelings, hearts. Everyone will get to tell their story, and then we will make a plan as to how things will be repaired. You'll be given a chance to make things right."

In the restorative model, it's not about who's to blame and what punishment is needed, but rather, what is the impact of certain behaviours and what remedy is needed.

Here's an example of an altercation between young siblings, Jenny (4) and Mandy (1), which was resolved restoratively by their mother. After Jen hit her little sister on the head with a plastic spade, Mum came over and took the crying child in her arms.

"Jenny, what happened?"

"Mandy keeps taking my spade, so I hit her on the head."

"But Jen, can you see Mandy is crying and very sad and sore? In our family we don't hit each other. Is there something you can get to make Mandy feel better? I promise after that we'll look at what happened and make a plan for you too. But we don't hit each other in this family."

Mum suggested that Jen go and get Mandy's sippy-cup from the kitchen, which she did, glad to be part of solving the problem.

Mum: "Is there anything else that might help to make her feel better? Do you want to give her a kiss?"

Jenny: "But Mum, Mandy was being so annoying. She wouldn't give me my spade."

Mum: "I understand. But hitting her on the head is not going to make things better. We can't just hit each other when things don't go our way. So here is my idea. Let's see what we can do so that Mandy starts to understand how to share or give something back to you that is yours. If she takes one of your things, try and find a replacement for her. Give her another toy, and then gently try to switch and take yours back. It may not work right away. Have patience and I'll show you. We will help her understand how to trade, because right now she's very little and she doesn't understand. Eventually she will get the idea. I will help you. But if you grab your stuff away from her and hit her on the head, then that's what she will do later, and that always ends up with someone crying."

Here's a story of two brothers, Liam and Brody, told by their father, John, as an example for working with older children.

"The boys were always fighting, and I used to really lose my temper at them," John said. "I didn't think there was another way, to be honest. But my wife and I told the boys that we were going to be doing things a bit differently at home, and wouldn't punish the boys or shout but try to work things out first. After a bit of a bumpy start, here's an example of how it worked, when Liam (10) recently took

Brody's (9) radio-controlled car and threw it into the hedge. I asked Brody if he'd be willing to have a chat about this – a restorative one – and try to fix this. He said yes. I waited until they weren't so angry – since you can't have any kind of conversation when kids are still fighting or angry. They just want to beat each other up. So, once they agreed to fix the situation this way, our conversation went something like this:

Dad: 'Liam, what happened?'

Liam: 'I threw Brody's car into the hedge. But he's been stealing my things all morning.'

Dad: 'What were you thinking?'

Liam: 'I was annoyed because he's been doing stuff to irritate me all morning.'

Dad: 'I understand. We will come back to that after. But let's fix the car throwing first. What do you think about this now?'

Liam: 'Well, it doesn't fix the problem. But I was frustrated.'

Dad: 'Brody, what happened?'

Brody: 'Liam threw my car into the hedge, and I can't find it.'

Dad: 'What's been the worst of that for you?'

Brody: 'I spent all my pocket money on it, and now I'm scared he broke it.'

Dad: 'What do you need in order to make things right?'

Brody: 'I need Liam to find it and, if it's broken, to fix it.'

Dad: 'Liam, does that sound fair to you? What can you offer to do in order to make that situation right?'

Liam: 'I'll get the car and fix it if I can or pay for a new one. But he did eat my chocolate.'

Dad: 'Thanks, Liam. We'll come back to that. Meanwhile, Brody, is that an acceptable solution?'

Brody: 'Sure.'

Liam: 'I'll go find the car. I'm sorry for what I did.'

Brody: 'Okay.'

Dad: 'Thanks, boys. We'll chat about the chocolates now, Brody, okay? And after maybe let's come up with some suggestions as to how we can make sure these fights stop happening.'"

The boys resolved that conflict. "It takes time," the dad said. "I can't say it's as quick as sending someone to their room, but I've noticed a change in their relationship and it's definitely helped family stress levels. Also, they're much quicker now to admit to what they've done, because they don't get punished, and the situation is resolved faster."

Being a restorative and affirmative parent is not the same as being a permissive parent who steps in and prevents kids from meeting their own responsibility to the world.

This is relationship-building.

When things go wrong, we can look at this nexus of dissonance as an opportunity for growth – to deepen understanding. Human relationships are infinitely complex. Kindness and honesty and listening go a long way to building grounded, healthy human connections.

There are no perfect families. No perfect relationships. Everything is in process. Every minute we are offered a number of potential pathways as to how something might pan out, depending on how we, as parents and caregivers, handle the situation.

Restorative practice is not magic fairy dust and it will not change your home overnight. But given time, there can be dramatic shifts. It is a worthy investment and can be the one thing that helps build trust and warmth between family members and allows everyone to deal with messy situations – situations which will always happen – in a measured and low-stress way.

Love Instead of Fear

In order to make children feel that they are part of a magnificent world, we advocate starting with valuing nature. When our children are small, stop the mad rush from one thing to the next. Take the time to look at butterflies and worms and bugs. Have a small patch of garden or balcony where things can grow. Care for a plant, or a pot of herbs; sprout a seed, grow a seedling. The simplest things that cost nothing can allow our kids to feel grounded in the world they inhabit. Play and laugh together. Build healthy nervous system responses. If our kids feel connected to a circle of loving people, if they feel connected to the natural world, they will value one another and other humans, and if they treasure nature, they will preserve it. We do not have to terrify our young children to "behave or else" – nor do we need to turn them into revolutionaries.

If we do this, when they reach their teens or early adulthood and they feel passionate about doing something about anything in their world, they will look for the positive impact they can make. We need to show them the value of putting energy into things that improve and enhance their lives and the lives of others.

It is our job to provide them with a sense of belonging and meaning and to give them a sense of the value of relationships.

How to Deal with Social Media

How do we cope with what happens to our children through social media? How do we protect them when the long arms of anything dubious can enter their world once our kids are connected to the internet? Remember the warnings from the previous chapter. Screens and social media are likely doing far more harm than good. We can protect them for a while, but soon we will not be able to prevent them from accessing many disturbing things in the world that can find them via their screens. We need to monitor their screen use. We also need to support them in other ways – show them that there is space for their friendships and their relationships at home.

Margaret told her son Carlton that he would not be able to have a phone until he was 13. This became harder and harder, as his friends would be connecting outside of school and he wasn't. She did what she could. She and her partner took her son and his friends out on a boating trip on a Saturday every few weeks. They had a barbecue. They had a good time and made sure the youngsters were engaged doing outdoor things and having a space. She did her best to ensure they built community. It requires some dedication of time and commitment to organise an excursion or an afternoon of teens at home, but again, it's an investment in their future. It sounds like such a simple thing it would be obvious to most of us – these are things we have always done – but increasingly these important moments are getting lost in the haze of screens.

It is not unusual at dinner time to find a family with three small children on various screens. Even parents will be on their screens – checking for that last email, getting the recipe for dinner on a phone. It's difficult to imagine life without screens, but if we don't teach our children how to live without them, they will have a hard time doing so later as adults.

And just because it's pervasive, doesn't mean it's innocuous. Being on screens creates a number of significant impacts on children's and teen's bodies and brains as they sit, immobile, staring into cyberspace. We know this is not ideal, and yet we keep doing it. If you have forgotten the warnings from the last chapter, simply remember this: all manner of healthy development comes from relationships in real time with real people. Time on screens displaces those opportunities regardless of age. From birth to death, people need people to grow, thrive and survive in a healthy and holistic fashion. And while there are many ways to counter the stresses that come up – because stresses are just the product of fear or other negative emotions in most scenarios – one of the most important is to be present in real time with real people. The answer to the disconnect that is often the precursor to things going wrong in relationships, behaviour and the way of the world lies obviously in *how we connect*.

So, we suggest these important countermeasures to a cyber-life or an existence permeated by fear and anxiety about the state of the world:

First, *connect to nature* in whatever way possible. As parents of young children, it is your responsibility to make time to connect them to the fresh air. Whether you live in a cold climate, in an apartment or on a farm, there is always some way to get fresh air. Get out there. The more time children spend in nature connecting to the earth and the sky and the ocean, the more their nervous systems are balanced.

Being in nature regulates blood flow and heart rhythms. It balances the nervous system and connects us to ourselves – more so when we are barefoot.[44] In fact, a study showed that walking barefoot is a "viable and low-cost activity to facilitating greater feelings of nature connectedness and psychological restoration". We are all time-poor, but this is an investment that we cannot afford not to make.

The same goes for teens. When Jim was 15 and came home from school, he would go straight onto his phone. Even though this was convenient for his single mother, at a certain point just before dinner, or sometimes just after, she would say, "Let's go for a walk or a bike ride." Sometimes they spent an hour, sometimes only 15 minutes. The point was, they were connecting. It's not the quantity but the quality of time spent that matters. That small window was a precious time of laughter, connection and joy.

The second countermeasure is therefore *connect to people*. Even if we are in the presence of our children much of the day, it's important to make time to give a child our undivided, unattached-to-a-screen attention. This could be half an hour before bed – a story, a game, some jokes. It could be a chat about funny things that happened today or highlights and lowlights of the day.

Parental interest and engagement are so important. As our kids get older, they don't appreciate questions like "How was your day?" Also, "Have you done your homework?" is not the kind of query that builds connection. Instead, genuine interest builds connection. When Laurie asked her 16-year-old about his science project to design an efficient wing, he talked for hours, teaching her about lift and drag, what a vortex is and how to optimise lift.

This builds connection, understanding, respect.

In summary, with small children, be involved. Engage in imaginative play. Laugh. With tweens and teens, be engaged but not suffocating. Remember that you are not a buddy – you are a parent. Hold that line.

As a parent, it is also important to bear in mind that sometimes teenagers want to disappear – into their rooms, their worlds. If they know that you're available for them, if they know there is no compulsion, a night walk around the block or a card game may actually appeal to them. But if it doesn't, don't worry or create stress around it. Don't give up though. Reach out later, the next day. Leave breathing room. Sometimes connecting with teens means watching their FAIL cat videos on YouTube and laughing for five minutes. Time spent together doesn't have to always be direct. In one family we know, rummy became a favourite. Every night the card game involved two parents and three children and lots of laughter. These simple things mitigate against the constant fear-mongering and against the social media monster that threatens to devour our children's lives and make them into zombies.

We understand how convenient it is when our children are seen and not heard as they enter the cyber world. Sometimes exhausted parents need a break. Within our own parenting, *Finding Nemo* was a godsend. But the internet is different and is not a dead space that our kids inhabit. Let's imagine children are playing a game, even a game that is not violent. As they succeed or fail, their heart rates speed up, they secrete adrenaline, perhaps cortisol. They are being corralled into a host of physiological responses that are completely invisible to anyone looking at them. Not to mention the fact, as noted in the previous chapter, that such games are designed to create an addictive, drug-like dependence through the way they trigger dopamine hits. So, although your child is not actually ingesting any substance, their bodies is producing dopamine. And that dopamine hit is addictive. Consequently, when you turn off the game or take away the item that is creating the feel-good feeling, withdrawal symptoms will result. In younger children this may lead to temper tantrums. In older children it may result in anger or resentment, and because their nervous systems are developing, what we are creating is dependency on devices and the need to get a daily fix. So, when we do turn to an iPad or a video or a series of funny movies, we should understand that all evidence points to this not having any benefits for young children and few benefits for older children. It may benefit the parent who needs a break because it creates a space, perhaps of silence, where they are able to get on with what they need to get on with. But we should acknowledge that this is for us, rather than for our children. Being a parent does take effort. We do have to look after ourselves, but we can't lose sight of why we do what we do and what the long-term effects might be.

If there is one point we wish to make to the parent who wants to be "grounded" – who wants to have kids who will survive emotionally, physically and psychologically in whatever the world throws at them next, here are some "off-road" thoughts. Perhaps these are self-evident, but sometimes the simple stuff points us back to the rough, winding road of reality. Being aware of the moment is so important:

You cannot connect to your small child once they are a teenager.

That ship has sailed.

You cannot connect to your teenager once they are an adult. So, all the things we do while our children are small are precious and cannot be replaced. We cannot go back through time and rectify things – though we can always make efforts to heal the past and resolve things that didn't go as we might have wanted them to go, with great benefit. But if we're present and grounded enough in the moment, we can do things that minimise damage later on. If the most important thing is love and connection for our children's flourishing, we should make sure that there is a conscious effort towards creating that. To do that, we ourselves need to be grounded, cared for, valued and coherent – so that our reactions are measured, loving, and as much as possible, connected.

Quantity is not quality. It doesn't have to be hours and hours. But when that connection time is there, it needs to be dedicated. We can't be staring at our screens while having a conversation absent-mindedly with a child of any age (and let's confess, all of us have done that!). Even as partners, we need to model what we wish to see in our children by allowing them to see that we connect with each other, that we value time together. In modern families it is often the case that even mealtimes now are not times of togetherness. Everybody grabs what they need when they need it. Kids eat watching their iPads or their phones. The amount of time that we spend looking into one another's eyes, sharing a joke, playing a game, has diminished. If we want the next generation to be compassionate, grounded, and not prone to overactive nervous systems, then we need to go in the opposite direction to that which the media wants us to go in – namely, a diet of constant fear, making us worry about everything from what we eat to the plight of the planet to being abducted or terrified of failing exams. We also need to beware of all the screen games that induce a fight-or-flight response. We can enable young minds and hearts to be safe havens for kids to retreat to when the world is overwhelming in what it offers and demands.

As children grow, discuss the pros and cons of social media and all things they are exposed to on screens. Be curious. It is very difficult to be punitive to big teenagers who are much smarter than we are at getting what they want. Your role as a parent changes as your children mature, and sometimes – in fact most of the time –we are behind the curve. We need to be aware when these changes happen so that we gradually go from being an all-knowing, all-powerful, beloved parent in their eyes to being a guide who will be there for them when they need us – but to clarify, we are still the parent as long as we are their guardian and they live under our roof. We are the adults and we do make the decisions.

Hold the parental line with grace and humour. It will all be worth it.

Ground Rules

1. Choose love instead of fear as the basis for engaging with your kids around world issues. This will support healthy nervous system development.

2. Praise effort and endeavour (social, academic, physical) rather than results or "smarts" to build self-worth and a sense of validity in our kids.

3. Focus on repairing and restoring rather than resorting to blaming and punishing. Over the long term, this builds relationships, connection and trust and allows for growth and transformation.

4. Make time to connect to one another. It is impossible to go back in time and do things over again, so value the moments.

Eight

Taking Care of Yourself Is Not Selfish

"What we are teaches the child far more than what we say, so we must be what we want our children to become."

– Joseph Chilton-Pearce[45]

Why You Put on Your Own Oxygen Mask First Before Helping Others

The same things we do that are essential for our children's health are also essential for ours: reduce stress; spend time away from screens; connect with others; spend time in nature; get exercise and oxygen; laugh... and getting the odd massage would not go amiss either!

It is easy to be hijacked by anxiety and stress as a parent in today's crazy world. But this does not make us better parents, nor does it make us more noble, more committed, or more functional. In fact, if we want our kids to be relaxed, resilient and proactive rather than reactive as they develop, we need to take care of ourselves so that we model these dispositions.

The good news is that, in doing so, we give ourselves a better chance of being healthier and happier in the long run. We are also able as a result to be more responsive in a measured and loving way when we face the inevitable series of meltdowns, arguments, tantrums, disagreements and all the hard stuff that is part of the unique parenting road each of us travels.

You are your child's entire environment when they are very young. And you continue to be an important component of their environment, which you help create, when they're older. Therefore, the most important things we give to our children are profoundly straightforward: love, care, acknowledgement, engagement, space. You, and the environment you create, have a direct impact on your child's brain, mind and future. Relationships literally shape your child's brain. An environment that is empathic, stress-free, loving and tender creates a very different brain, and by association future, than an environment that is anxious, cold, inconsistent or harsh.[46] And while it's easy to get swept away by the thought that providing our children with amazing stuff, enrolling them in every type of program, and buying special toys will set them up for what we think of as "success", ultimately, the most important element in your child's environment is YOU.

So, you need to take care of you.

You might not be able to control all the things that happen around you and hold back all the unexpected things that fall from the sky and mess up perfectly good days or plans or weeks. What you can do, however, is look at yourself as the most precious thing in your child's world.

It's impossible to control how much sleep you get and how busy your days are, but there are a few things that you can always do that will impact the environment that your kids grow up in. If you're reading this book, then it's obvious that you are one of those parents who cares enough to want to be the best parent and person and give your child the best start in life. But in order to do that, you need to survive (and thrive) on this off-road journey, which is unique to each family and does not come with a detailed map or "how-to" manual.

Caring for ourselves means starting with caring for our nervous systems. How do we do this?

The Quick Coherence Technique

Shelley is a certified HeartMath Coach and Mentor. For the past 15 years she has helped hundreds of parents, teachers, students (and herself) to get off the "stress freeway" and keep nervous systems balanced.

The two-minute Quick Coherence Technique developed by the Institute of HeartMath is a tool which we can all have at our disposal and which can balance the autonomic nervous system, stopping a fight-or-flight stress response in its tracks.

If we care for ourselves and our nervous systems, this will influence the way we parent; in other words, it will have an effect on our children's environment. Everyone wins!

Airplane safety briefings always ask us to first put on our own masks so we have oxygen before helping a child or someone less able put on theirs. This is an overused metaphor, but it is not out of place here, because when your nervous system is balanced and you are not in fight-or-flight, your response to whatever is happening will be more balanced and regulated. This in turn creates children whose own stress responses are less likely to be overreactive. Not only that: you are having an effect on your own body that is positive and supports better health.

How not to overreact is an important part of parenting. For example, if your two-year-old knocks a cup of milk off the table and you yell at him, he will get a terrible fright; he will feel bad; his stress response will be activated – even though, in all honesty, this is not a situation worthy of a parental melt-down. There is no doubt that there are times in life when we do need to use the blood-curdling scream: if your two-year-old runs out into the road, then you must yell at the top of your lungs. If something dangerous is threatening your child, then you are justified to go full fight-or-flight. But using that for spilled milk or when kids run and don't walk as you asked them to, for example, is not necessary. If you have a marked stress response in situations that do not really warrant the expenditure of so much energy, you will not only wear yourself out but will run the risk of amplifying your child's stress response and either making them deaf to your screams or setting them up to be overreactive. Don't, if possible, freak them out.

By now we have hopefully made it clear that the heart and brain are intricately connected, and that this relationship impacts the entire body – every system, every process. Feeling love and appreciation is a powerful shifter of physiological states. Your thoughts and emotions, therefore, are your most potent instruments. Every thought, every feeling affects how your heart functions and therefore how your nervous system responds. Is your heart racing with stress/fear or filled with love/gratitude? Are you full of cortisol and norepinephrine (adrenaline) with nowhere to run? Are you feeling positive and happy and loving? Thankfully, these are the elements over which you have some degree of control, no matter what is happening around you.

Here are some practical steps to follow so that you have enough metaphorical oxygen flowing to you to be able to help those around you.

Step one is to get yourself into a physiological state that is optimum. Breathwork, meditation and yoga all offer that benefit over time. You can then add something that can be done without going anywhere and in the midst of a busy life: HeartMath's Quick Coherence Technique.

Focus your attention on the area of your heart. Put your hand there, if you like. Breathe in and out a little bit slower and deeper than you usually do. Maybe count slowly to five as you breathe in and to six as you breathe out. Then, thinking about something or someone you care about deeply, allow yourself to feel deep appreciation, love or gratitude for this something or someone. Do this for two minutes.

Add to that the words "inner ease" and focus on the response to these words.

That's it. That's one small step to help stay grounded.

Do this every day, every morning and evening. Extend the time you do this each day and build a new baseline that is calmer and less reactive. You can also call on this as you feel tempers or negative emotions rising. What you are doing is getting the autonomic nervous system into balance. You are stopping the fight-or-flight runaway train that happens with an overactive sympathetic nervous system. You are tuning your instrument (you) – and now you can reach out and hold the toddler who is melting down or speak to the sullen teenager – and at the very least, you will not be pouring petrol onto a smouldering fire.

The Institute of HeartMath has shown, using sensitive magnetometers, how the heart's electromagnetic field extends for more than 1 metre (3 feet) around each of us, carrying sensitive electromagnetic information from our hearts which can then impact and be received by others. In the diagram below from the Institute of HeartMath, the reach of the heart's electromagnetic field is shown.[47]

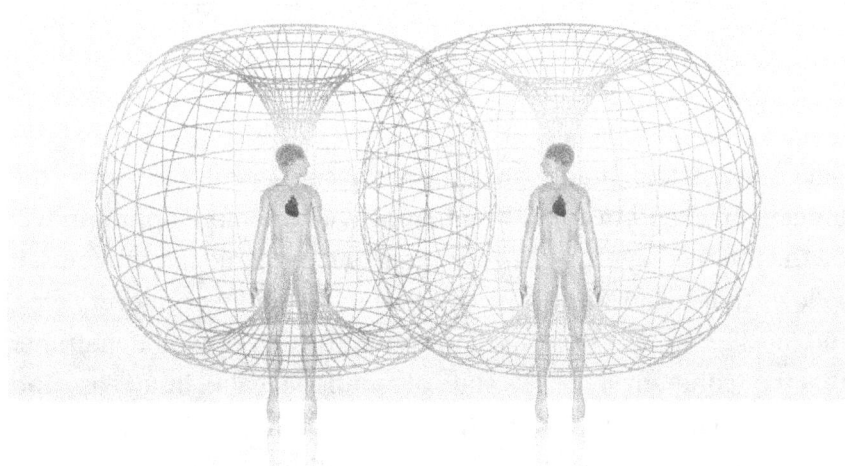

The next diagram shows one person's ECG (electrocardiogram or heart-rate pattern) time-locked to another person's EEG (electroencephalogram or brain-wave pattern) for a short while. According to the Institute of HeartMath, this indicates that when two people are at conversational distance, the electromagnetic signal generated by one person's heart may influence another person's brain rhythms. Simply put: feeling love and appreciation can enhance not only our own but another's brain function. If we are "coherent" and loving, we not only reduce our own stress but can also have a physiological effect on others.[48]

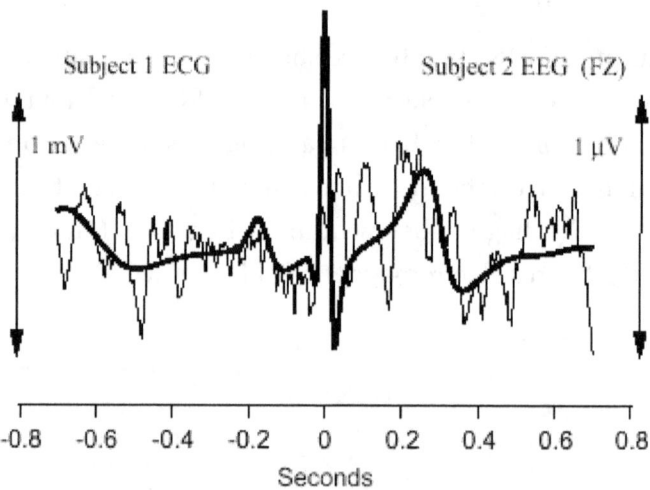

Since hearts and brains are intricately connected, and since the longer you spend in a highly coherent state the more optimum will be the interacting physical, emotional and psychological systems, it follows that if you want your children to be geniuses in every way, the most important step is to show them you love them! Remember that the "coherent state" is a state of emotional calm, inner ease and balance. When in that state, the body becomes efficient. Systems become balanced, harmonious. This is then represented by the patterns made by a person's heartbeat, which look more organised and form a sine wave.

The Quick Coherence Technique gets you there quickly. A "coherent" heart rate variability (HRV) pattern (blue in the diagram below) differs from an "incoherent" one. When feeling stressed, our fight-or-flight response generates a ragged and disorganised pattern (red).[49] This is great for getting us out of immediate danger. It's not so great if it becomes the way our bodies are most of the time. That is then a place of chronic stress from which no good things come.

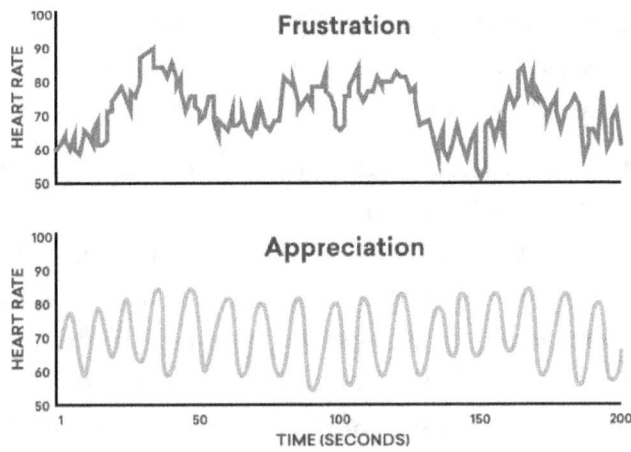

The Coherent State

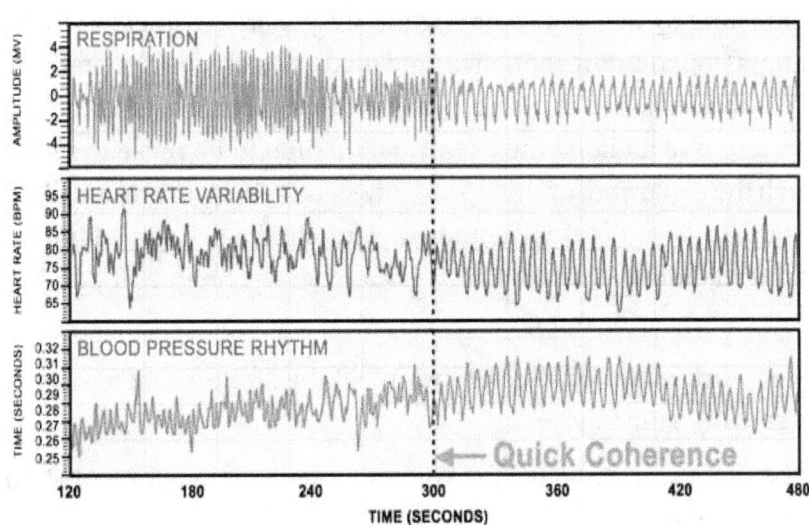

When you practice the Quick Coherence Technique, respiration, blood pressure and HRV change significantly (see diagram on previous page).

If we create environments in which our children experience love, gratitude and appreciation, we will ensure they grow up feeling secure, confident, appreciative, and emotionally stable. This is the biggest gift we can give them. Creating such an environment similarly gives us the biggest gift we could possibly want as parents: the physical, emotional and psychological dispositions to be the best version of ourselves we can be. So, how do we do that? By supporting ourselves physically, emotionally and psychologically.

Here are some scenarios: your three-year-old child is having a meltdown in the middle of a supermarket. He's screaming and the object that he wants is suddenly life and death to him, but you've said no, and you're trying to stand by what you said. You are tempted to give in, but the reality is that by saying no you are not a bad person and you do not have to give in, even if it looks like the line of least resistance to an exhausted soul. Stick to your no, gently and lovingly. Breathe in deeply and focus on *not letting your cortisol level go up*.

Screaming back at a screaming child or losing it and dragging them along by the arm or hitting them (scenarios witnessed by the authors) is counterproductive and makes everyone feel terrible. This is the response of a tired person with no more patience, and of course, we've all been there. Now is the time to be present; as you watch the explosion, or the storm, stay steady. The world is not about to end as a result of this meltdown. Your child will not be damaged by this meltdown. Do the Quick Coherence Technique. If possible, speak calmly with your child.

Here is an example witnessed by one of the authors when a parent got caught in the fray:

The setting: supermarket checkout. Characters: Mum, boy of about 4, girl of about 6.

Something happens. Both children are crying. The girl cries loudest and pulls on her distracted mother's sleeve.

> Girl: Mum, he hit me!
>
> Mum: What? Joshua, come here this minute!
>
> Mum grabs Josh roughly, slams his hand onto the handle of the shopping trolley and holds it there. He sobs like the world is ending and kicks his mother.
>
> Mum: You do NOT hit your sister! You do NOT kick me!
>
> Boy (sobbing): But she kicked me in the FACE first!

Both children end up shouting and crying, and Mum is ironically yelling above them to please SHUT UP to gain peace and calm!

Most of us have been there – or somewhere near there – sometime. Firstly, we have to forgive ourselves. We are not perfect all the time, and sometimes this kind of scenario unfolds before we even realise what is going on. Imagine if we were prepared – if we had the presence of mind to take 30 seconds to focus our attention on breathing, to draw on the Quick Coherence Technique. Then, perhaps a short, restorative conversation might not have made the situation worse. The more awareness we have of our physical state, the more presence of mind we can have to be measured and fair in the face of the wild hurricanes. Then we are more likely to be able to address situations calmly when they do go pear-shaped.

Being in a coherent state in the face of a meltdown may not end the tantrum/fight/explosion, but it will help to avoid amplifying the situation. The same goes for situations where our tweens or teens might start being argumentative and pushing back against the boundaries we set, testing the limits in ways that can easily trigger us. Remember that the teen brain is a work in progress and more likely to engage in highly charged emotional behaviours because its frontal lobes are not very good at putting the brakes on those feelings when it matters.

A colleague's 17-year-old son recently ran his mother's car into the neighbour's BMW while reversing out of the drive without looking.

She was devastated, but before even talking to him, she spent a while just breathing herself into a calm state. Then, using a restorative approach, she told him firstly she was so glad he was okay, and then she asked him what had happened. When he told her, she said she understood that these things happen and asked him what he thought he could do to make good. He offered to pay for all costs not covered by insurance with the money he earned working at a pizza place on weekends. She asked him what he thought he could do to ensure a similar accident didn't happen again, and he said it was definitely a wake-up call and he would be super-aware while driving from now on and ensure he checked his surroundings before reversing.

The potential stress of this situation was mitigated by the low-stress response, which in no way "let him off the hook" but ensured that neither mother nor son were given any more anxiety than that which was already there as a result of the incident. This is all-round good news for everyone's nervous systems. For parents, it's particularly important to understand that we do this not only for our children but also for our relationships and for ourselves and our own health.

It is easy to be triggered into fight-or-flight. What if your teenager is rude to you? You can be rude back, but is that going to help them learn to be a better person? Perhaps it would be helpful to stop them in their tracks and say, "You know, when you say XYZ, it is very hurtful. It's also unwarranted. I understand you are feeling tired. I am too, but let's not resort to hurtful words that we might regret saying. Your words do have an impact, so can we do our best to find another way? Let's talk about this in a little while when both of us have taken a few deep breaths."

Sometimes we too do the wrong things. Both of the authors of this book have said things or responded to kids in less than optimum ways in hindsight – we are, after all, only human. Sometimes, things do go badly. Our parental nervous systems get out of whack, and our responses are not measured or coherent. It is not impossible that you, as a loving parent, might find yourself one day turning into the wicked witch of the north.

But there is always a way back from there.

Show your kids how to be. Show them how to apologise. Breathe in. Give yourself a second chance. Give your kids/partner/spouse a second chance.

Who we are is the most important element in our children's immediate environment.

Once the storm has passed, you can apologise for anything you did or said that you regret.

One of the authors has said something close to this on several occasions: "I'm so sorry I was so grumpy with you this morning. I was very tired and stressed about other things and I overreacted to your comment. I'm sorry for how I responded. I hope you understand that I love you and did not mean to cut you off or be short with you. That was not warranted or okay."

You do not lose face. You do not lose your authority as a parent – which is often an underlying fear. You are showing your kids how to be an honest, compassionate, and of course, flawed human being.

You are showing them also how to forgive themselves and make good when they do regrettable things.

Give them the blueprint for the behaviour you wish them to exhibit.

Keep steady. Generate a coherent heart rhythm as soon as you are able to.

This is your oxygen.

Then you are available to help others.

No one is perfect and we all mess things up.

This is part of caring for yourself as a parent.

Fill Up Your Tank

Many of us feel guilty, once we've been parenting for a few years, when we take precious time away from our children to care for ourselves – to do things that perhaps seem superficial or non-essential.

A recent observation by a 75-year-old grandmother might give parents an encouraging picture. She noted in a conversation that she was astonished at the level of self-care exhibited by a pair of kookaburras: they preened and dived into a bird-bath and cleaned their feathers and cleaned one another's feathers, over and over again. The level of dedication given to this act of self-care by these beautiful creatures was second to none. We might consider this when thinking about things that seem non-essential indulgences and yet give us a sense of being cared for ourselves, being looked after. Getting a massage, getting one's hair done, or going for a swim or to the gym or for a walk are activities that give us a sense of well-being. These activities allow us to breathe out, physically and metaphorically. If we do things that sustain us, we gain strength, we increase our capacity to manage stress, and we are less likely to "lose it".

Easier said than done, we know.

And yet this is a vital part of parenting. It should, in our opinion, be a priority.

It's important, too, that kids see that the adults around them do things for themselves that bring them joy. Your children should see you making time for other adults and see that you love doing yoga, going for a run, painting, playing music, fixing a car or computer. They should see you honouring yourself and your needs and giving yourself loving attention as you honour them and give them loving attention. Your going to a singing lesson or a dance class or seeing a friend or having half an hour of "quiet time" even just once a week is something that not only fills your tank but shows your kids that you value yourself.

And what is this "self"?

Here's the tricky part. When you are a parent, it's easy to take on the role of just being someone's mum or dad. Spouses even start to call each other "Mum" or "Dad". We recommend being aware of the way this can undermine your ability to be another self, not just the loving parent, but the partner who has a sense of humour, the professional, the friend who laughs at dad jokes, the aunty to whom nieces confess their secrets, the uncle who teaches his nephew how to fly or play the guitar.

If we want to parent fully and give our kids the best of ourselves, it's our contention that we need to be, as much and as soon as possible, the fullness of all aspects of ourselves – and to allow our kids to see at least some of those selves in action. We could even say that it is important to be selfish and do things for yourself. Feeling good allows you to help others feel good.

Being your best, happiest self for as much of the time as you can, loving and honouring yourself as you love and honour your children, gives them the best chance of being happy and healthy at every stage of development.

Focus on being present, coherent.

If you lose control, acknowledge this, and recalibrate.

A recent study has found that happy people live statistically longer lives than unhappy people. Consider this for a moment. The researchers discuss that the correlation is complex and suggest that happy people live longer because they are healthier – but why? The paper does not explore the impact of feeling joy on physiology. They touch on ideas that being healthy allows people to feel happier and, conversely, happier people might make healthier lifestyle decisions.[50] In fact, feeling gratitude, love and appreciation sets off a cascade of renewing and repairing physiological processes, while feeling anxiety/stress sets off a cascade of depleting processes as the body gears itself towards what should be a short-term fight-or-flight event. There is the distinct possibility that the physiological impact of feeling joy/happiness/gratitude as opposed to stress and sadness has far-reaching effects. The Institute of HeartMath cites the following: "Positive emotions are a reliable predictor of better health, even for those without food or shelter while negative emotions are a reliable predictor of worse health even when basic needs like food, shelter and safety are met."[51]

Making joy a focal point of the parenting journey will stand everyone in good stead. Living a happy and long and healthy life is likely the goal of almost every living being – and ensuring that our children live long, happy, healthy lives is without a doubt the wish of every loving parent.

So, after ensuring we know how to get into a state of high coherence, and how to manage issues that are stressful without losing our minds, and ensuring we take care of ourselves in small and significant ways even when time is tight and the ability to get five minutes' peace might be next to impossible – how can we create environments of joy that sustain the whole family? Here are a few suggestions.

Finding Joy Through Family Games and Exercises

1. Rose and Thorn Exercise for Building Family Connection

Once a week, have the family sit together after or before dinner around the table and allow each person from age three upwards to share: what was their rose and what was their thorn? The rose is something beautiful or inspiring that happened in the week, and the thorn is something that maybe wasn't so nice or was a bit of a challenge. No one says anything to anyone's rose and thorn, except "Thank you". This is a ritual that builds connection, a sense of love, trust, and a sense of what is happening for each member of the family. One of the authors learned about this and saw it in action at a dinner where an extended family and friends on a Friday evening shared their roses and their thorns. The youngest sharer was 3, and the oldest was 75. It took a little while, but at the end everyone was feeling warm and connected.

2. Birthday Books

At least once every couple of years, instead of buying cards and writing brief messages in them and then wondering what to do with the cards, or needing to throw them away, create a birthday book for each person. This book gets filled up prior to the birthday with drawings, messages and wishes from friends and family who might be coming to a celebration. People can send their messages by email, via text, or write them in the book on the day. Then the book is wrapped up and becomes one of the presents. It is a beautiful way of creating something that has meaning for all times. It costs nothing, takes hardly any more time than buying and writing a card, and yet has enormous value for the receiver, regardless of their age. Over time, a collection of these books can be very precious for the people who receive them, showing them what people appreciate and love about them through time. This is something that is nice to do every few years – not necessarily every year – and the joy it brings cannot be underestimated.

3. Jokes and Games

The other element that we have not yet talked about is humour. By humour, we don't mean sarcasm or putting people down, or making jokes at others' expense. This is not about satire. Getting joy out of our children's jokes and antics requires us to be in the present moment, to look at the world through their eyes and to see things from their point of view as much as possible. Laughing together allows for deep connection and bonding. Share jokes – even bad dad jokes. Allow your kids to have their moment, their punchline. Give the three-year-old your full attention when she tells her made-up knock-knock jokes. There is no end to the value of a good laugh. Play games. It's always a rather interesting question to ask other parents and adults when they stopped playing. And by playing, we don't mean competitive sports, but the kinds of games that create laughter and joy, like tag, stuck-in-the-mud, cat and mouse, or duck-duck-goose.[52]

As teacher educators, we have done our fair share of playing these games with adults, and the most incredible – or perhaps not incredible – thing is that adults enjoy playing as much as – if not more than – the children that they are going to teach. Perhaps our serious lives make us crave laughter and fun in a much more serious fashion! It is an odd thing that we stop playing at a certain point, but the playful side of us is easily reawoken. One of the benefits of having children is that we have a good excuse to play again and get joy out of it.

We have seen adults shrieking with delight as they pursue each other in a game of cat and mouse. There is nothing manufactured about the joy – and the physical exercise and oxygen that we get, as well as a sense of connection and shared hilarity in a single simple game, costs nothing and may be a factor in allowing us to live longer, happier, healthier lives. Even teenagers who think that playing is uncool can be co-opted into such games.

Shelley has organised hopscotch games for teenagers with massive hopscotch squares that presented a wonderful challenge for any young adult. The games became quite competitive, but the fact that the hopscotch squares were in fact in the shape of a giant bunny, and the stones they used were odd-shaped rather than aerodynamic, took the edge off the play and added humour.

Hide and seek is a great family game. So is "sardines" – a variation of the hide-and-seek game requiring more than four players for maximum fun. You can find the rules for sardines via google.

These are just some suggestions that any parent can take on board tomorrow in as small or big a way as they wish.

The pathways to joy, to creating positive environments and reducing stress, are mostly remarkably simple. We know we are not saying anything very new here – in fact, this is ancient knowledge. But the studies that tell us about the impact of joy and happiness on physiology, and the reality of our fast-paced and often inadvertently stressful lives, can get in the way of our ability to see things clearly.

We need to feel happy, well, loved and supported, and we deserve to. If we value ourselves, we are in a stronger position to support our children and to be there for them for a long time – enjoying every moment and facing the challenges with equanimity, courage and love so that, in time, our children will become adults who can do the same.

Ground Rules

1. You are the most important element in your child's environment.
2. Taking care of yourself means being in a better position to care for your children. Self-care is not selfish!
3. Practise the Quick Coherence Technique to immediately balance the autonomic nervous system.
4. Feeling happy is a predictor of living a longer, healthier life. Look for opportunities for joy in every encounter/situation.
5. Share, play games and laugh to create joy, well-being and connection in your home and in your relationships.

Nine

Nurturing a Healthy and Happy Mind

"It's all about the future isn't it? We work hard to get ahead in preparation for something better and we prepare our children for the future so they can get ahead. We want the best for our kids and too often this translates into having children do more sooner or finding ways to build their résumés earlier."

– Dr Michael C. Nagel[53]

Am I Doing the Right Thing for My Child?

More than a decade ago, the quote above appeared in one of Michael's books. At that time, he was doing a great deal of research and writing about child development and in particular brain development. You see, in a previous lifetime, Michael was a teacher, and in 1998 he became a parent for the first time. Needless to say, he not only had a professional interest in the topic but was also mindful of – or should we say scared to death of – the risk of being a "bad" parent. Despite all the advice he had received leading up to the birth of his daughter Madeline, holding her in his arms for the first time was both miraculous and terrifying!

Most parents can probably relate to the feelings Michael experienced. And most can likely relate to a question that tends to enter a parent's psyche repeatedly: am I doing the right thing for my child? Chances are you have asked yourself that question recently. That is a good thing – reflecting on what we do to and with our children is arguably the most important parenting skill. However, it is unlikely that anyone will ever find an absolute answer to such a question, because no two children are exactly alike. Even "identical" twins can show differences in temperament and other innate characteristics, so finding a template for perfect parenting is simply not possible. What is possible, however, is taking what we have learned from years of research in child development, education and psychology and adapting that to meet the needs of our own children. In this way we can ground ourselves in potential pathways for nurturing healthy and happy minds. This chapter looks to offer insights into the research noted earlier so that you can take whatever bits and pieces you find helpful and do all that you can to nurture your child in the best way for them – and for you. We will also focus on what can nurture your child outside the home and more specifically in school, but only after we look at what you can do as a parent.

First Thing – Mind the Mind!

Throughout this book we have paid attention to the impact of stress on you and your children. Perhaps a brief refresher of some key points is necessary to help our discussion.

First, child development is more marathon than sprint, especially in terms of the brain, which is not fully mature until we are in our twenties. This means there is plenty of opportunity for parents to help foster healthy development, especially during the early years and adolescence. It also means that the environment and experiences matter.

Second, anxiety and stress can lead to trauma and impact you and your child in untold ways if left unchecked. Having a healthy mindset and engaging in aspects of restorative practice help to counteract anxiety and stress. Relatedly, the point was made in Chapter 2 that parents want to protect their children but not at the expense of making them weak or vulnerable. Instead, we want to be resilient and instil that resilience in our children.

Third, resilience also forms the backdrop for coping in a world often embedded in messages of fear where the media thrives on making us anxious. Resilience is something fostered in real time with real people and likely diminished in virtual worlds where being "liked" requires little more than a well-timed and often enhanced photo of oneself or a version of one's life. So, what might be some other factors in shaping resilience and nurturing a healthy and happy mind? That is where this conversation begins.

Resilience Is...

If you were to look up the word resilience in a dictionary, you would see something to the effect that resilience is the capacity to withstand or recover quickly from difficulties; to have a degree of "toughness" or the ability to "bounce back" from adversity. The word "withstand" is an important one for parents to always keep in mind. We say this because many parents, too often, feel the need to fully protect their children from all the challenges they face or the fears they have.

In the last couple of decades much has been written about how some parents do all they can to make their children's pathway to adulthood as smooth and protected as possible. From "helicopter parents" (those who hover overhead and monitor every aspect of a child's life) to "snowplough parents" (those who seek to remove all obstacles from a child's path so they don't ever experience any pain, failure, or discomfort), and everything in between, there have been variations to parenting styles over the last couple of generations. Some of this is likely due to the constant bombardment of bad and fearful news on a 24/7 news cycle. Or it may be the case that the trend for having fewer and fewer children has meant parents could expend more time and energy on the day-to-day goings-on of their children. Truth be told, children are generally safer today than in any other generation, but our access to stories about terrible things happening to children has increased exponentially. We tend to agree with many researchers who argue that modern parenting is now wildly out of sync with the actual risks of growing up.[54] Whatever the label, and whatever the rationale, there are some things we can definitively say are not in the best interests of your child if you adopt an overzealous approach to protecting your child.

Trying to shield your child from anything bad in life might be making them more vulnerable to anxiety and stress-related disorders. The research in this area is clear. Parents who go out of their way to protect their children from failing or every possible risk that comes with being a child can create an exaggerated fear of situations that aren't risky at all. Living in fear, real or not, creates anxiety.

Risks, challenges and stressors are often a natural consequence of living. Rather than trying to shield or eliminate anything that might be in your child's way, help them to develop their own abilities to deal with life's challenges. It is worth noting that learning to face one's problems is not only an avenue for growth and learning but also a mechanism for building resilience. This is why helping children to learn to confront their fears and challenges is the best way to decrease their anxiety. This also relates to ensuring that children know that there is nothing wrong with failing from time to time and realising that a child's self-esteem is not enhanced by constant praise and gratuitous awards.

Failing Can Be Good for Your Child!

Over recent years, one of the most difficult things we have encountered as researchers and educators is convincing parents that failing and/or losing can be good for their child. We could speculate at length as to why that might be, but perhaps it comes down to a couple of points. First, our society has cultivated notions of the importance of winning and, at times, winning at all costs. Now don't get us wrong – we have no problem with winning. Winning feels good! Which leads to our next point: losing or failing feels bad! And increasingly our society has stigmatised losing while simultaneously doing everything possible to keep children out of harm's way. Such approaches are not helpful, for several reasons, but let's start by unpacking the merits of failing first.

Fail brilliantly! That is the title of one of Shelley's books – a book that she and co-author Dr Paul Williams wrote a few years back and one that has received great reviews and feedback from around the globe.[55] In their book, Shelley and Paul contend that not all failures are the same. The sinking of the *Titanic*, the unsinkable ship, is an example of a "first degree failure". First degree failures are typically catastrophic events beyond our control. "Second degree failures" are those that force us to hold our breath and hope for the best. Apollo 13 is an example. Although three astronauts managed to return to Earth safely after a major mechanical mishap, with the help of out-of-the-box thinking and using the moon to catapult them home, the mission itself was widely seen as a failure by those outside of NASA – no moon landing equalled failure. And finally, "third degree failures" are those that are personal and the result of the lines we (sometimes arbitrarily) draw in the sand – for example: A pass for this test is 80%. A pass for that test is 40%. Or, "I will consider myself a writer when I have published my first or fiftieth book". Thus, achieving 70% can lead to a person feeling like they are unworthy – while in another context, a mark of 50% leads to a feeling of success. In other words, different degrees of failure require different responses. We need to support our kids in such a way that their sense of self-worth is not unduly tied to the marks they receive, or the games that they win, or the many third-degree failures they will encounter. They (and we) need to be aware that a third-degree failure is merely an unwanted outcome – something we can learn from, grow from, move on from – and should not result in kids feeling suicidal because of a failed test.

It is important that our children have a sense of self-worth that does not attach too closely to metrics or standards. Third-degree failures are those that we all experience at various times in our lives. Schools are places where we often see these types of failures in terms of grades and performance. Tests, assignments and other performance measures can all result in a "fail". It is even possible for a child to fail his or her year and have to repeat it the next year under the softer expression of "being held back".

So what do all these types of failures have in common. Let's be clear! There is a huge difference between getting a bad grade and an ocean liner sinking to the bottom of the sea with many people dying in the process. But all degrees of failures present opportunities for growth and learning. And that is perhaps the best we can say, given, as Shelley and Paul rightly acknowledge in their book, society still frowns on failures and we still feel bad when we fail. But what we can do is help our children by acknowledging the feelings that come with failing, while also supporting notions of learning from our mistakes and growing from our frustrations, and understanding that we are not defined by the results of these kinds of failures.

Growth and learning – aren't those two things we want for all children? Failing is not fun and it is only the occasional masochist who finds pleasure in failing. But it is how we approach failing that matters. Wallowing in negative emotion is unhelpful and actually a great way to foster anxiety and stress. Helping your child understand that failures are temporary and opportunities for improvement helps to build resilience and a mindset for success – remember Chapter 7?

When looking at the debilitating aspects of fear, and particular the fear of failing, we noted the important work of Stanford University's Professor Carol Dweck. A quick refresher: Professor Dweck's research is all about "mindsets".[56] She has spent much of her career doing a tremendous amount of research aimed at understanding why some people give up in the face of challenge or adversity while others do everything they can to overcome it. She has found that what you believe is key. If a person believes that their skills or talents are inborn and fixed, they do what they can to avoid failure at all costs. Such individuals like to solve the same things repeatedly to reinforce a sense of competence. For example, children with a "fixed" mindset would rather do an easy puzzle and succeed than attempt something harder. They feel better and smarter when they get it right but often do not garner anything more than a warm fuzzy feeling. However, those who believe that skills and talents grow through effort and persistence see challenges and failures as opportunities to improve – as noted in Chapter 7, they have developed what is known as a "growth" mindset. Those who have a growth mindset feel smart when they're learning – and "failures" are seen as ways of discovering things that perhaps don't work but offer valuable opportunities for growth, evolution and new ideas.

Having a growth mindset is the goal, and it is our contention that fostering a growth mindset is an integral part of parenting. Significantly, doing so is not all that difficult. You can start by urging your child to try new things and take risks. They should also be encouraged to face challenges with a positive attitude and be taught the value of hard work. And at the risk of being repetitive, teach them to learn from their mistakes and not to overly ruminate on things that go wrong. These things are not only teachable moments when opportunities present themselves but are also something that you can model.

And finally, perhaps the most important thing for grounding your "nurturing parent" mindset is to always praise the effort and not the outcome. Effort is something that a person can control, but outcomes often rely on many other variables including the opinions and judgements of others. But be careful, because too much praise, or undeserved praise, can also create problems. Trophy day celebrations or school awards nights are often good examples of this – and of what not to do.

And the Award Goes to... !

One of the most problematic trends over the last couple of decades has been the misguided notion that the "self-esteem" of children is at risk if they never get an award. From this we have seen the emergence of trophy nights and school awards ceremonies where everyone gets a trophy or some form of recognition for simply showing up. It may sound cynical, but we have seen this repeatedly with our own children and through work-related activities. This practice is profoundly wrong, plain and simple. It also coincides with evidence noting that our perception of children as psychologically fragile is a quintessentially modern concept.[57] Children are more resilient than we might give them credit for as we try to protect them from feeling bad. Indeed, there isn't any evidence that the psyche of a child is damaged if they don't get an award and an abundance of research telling us why endlessly rewarding everyone is not a positive endeavour.

Let's start by acknowledging that self-esteem is important and that children are born with their self-esteem intact. The challenge is to avoid doing things that might have a negative impact on children's self-esteem – things like demonising failure, for example. It is equally important to note that from around the mid-1970s onwards we have seen an increasingly massive cottage industry devoted to self-esteem and spurious recommendations about how to build and care for a child's self-esteem. Assumptions that boosting self-esteem would lead to improvements in academic performance permeated the hallways of many schools, and as such self-esteem also became a central consideration for many educators. Some schools proclaimed that teachers would not mark in red pen, for example, lest the shock of a different and more obvious colour on a page harm a child's self-esteem. Some schools would even install mirrors with phrases like "you are now looking at a very special and wonderful person" engraved on them to help boost a child's self-esteem.

The problem with these seemingly good intentions is they are unlikely to do anything other than make the adults in charge feel good.

Many researchers have concluded that although the relationships between self-esteem and school performance might be somewhat noteworthy, the benefits are so small as to be not worth pursuing.[58] In fact, in trying to prop up a child's self-esteem with such activities, along with gratuitous praise, awards and trophies, adults might actually be diminishing motivation, creating unrealistic notions that everyone is a winner, or even worse, fostering narcissism.

The research on the negative outcomes on this matter is robust and extensive. For example, attempts to foster positive notions of self-esteem in children by giving everyone a trophy and telling them they are wonderful nurtures the type of fixed mindset we should be trying to avoid. If everyone is a winner, then there can never be a loser, nor can there be an opportunity to learn from those who excel. We know that human beings are often driven to do well when they aren't the best. We also know that losing, amid the excellence of another, is a learning opportunity, a chance to nurture a growth mindset by focusing on effort and what needs to be done to improve. Of further interest beyond the gazing eyes of researchers is that children, including infants, and teens are aware of when their peers are rewarded for doing nothing.

Learning to share is an important aspect of moral development, and children are provided with many opportunities to divide things equally. Social psychologists have studied what they refer to as distributive justice and the concept of proportionality in children and have found that by age six children already demonstrate a preference for rewarding the harder worker in a group. Even toddlers have demonstrated this by showing surprise when two people were given the same reward although only one of them did the work. At times children struggle with this intuition when it means they might get less of a reward, but by the time they reach adolescence they are better at applying proportionality to themselves.[59] Numerous studies have supported our understanding of proportionality and rewards in young people and have shown that *human beings innately favour fair distributions over equal ones* and do not respond well to "unfair equality". And despite the mountains of research suggesting otherwise, sporting clubs and schools often continue to give a trophy to everyone, which literally helps no one. The child who has excelled goes unrecognised, while all the others are afforded unfair equality. Remember, even a two-year-old can tell something isn't right when everyone gets the same reward, regardless of input.

We suspect that there may be some people reading this who are thinking that we are somewhat tyrannical and mean. On occasions, and despite the evidence presented, we have faced some parents who simply do not like our claims about trophies and rewards. All we ask is that if you are finding our proposition troubling, just look at the evidence. You won't have to look far to find that rewards for nothing, gratuitous and excessive praise, repeatedly telling a child how fantastic they are, and proclaiming that everyone is a winner never ends well in the real world. So much so that these approaches have also been linked to a range of troubling behaviours and mental health issues.

One of the most worrying trends we have seen resulting from the self-esteem industry and overzealous approaches to making all children feel special all the time is the link between putting children on a pedestal and narcissism. Praising children when they do good work or behave well is not the problem. However, heaping praise for the littlest of achievements or sometimes for poor performance, under the guise of enhancing positive self-esteem, is actually a recipe for narcissism. Treating children as "special" all the time leads to young people becoming too self-absorbed and fragile in the face of actual hard work and negative feedback. It also instils a sense of entitlement. If you are forever being told how great you are and rewarded for little, if any effort, then you start to believe that this should always be the case because you are special and deserve to be treated as such. We could go on, but we think you get the idea, and there are excellent resources you can explore further.[60] Praise your kids, but don't overdo it. Reward them for effort and when they achieve something of merit. And when things go wrong, don't focus on feelings but rather pay attention to actions for improvement. Making a plan of action helps build resilience, supports autonomy, nurtures a growth mindset and avoids ruminating over negative thoughts. Continually thinking of negatives leads to anxiety, so teach your child to take action and move forward. Movement, figuratively speaking, is good for the mind. Interestingly, literally moving the body is also good for the mind and one of the last things explored in the remainder of this chapter.

Activity and Mother Nature Nurture the Brain

In discussing some of the issues associated with screen devices in Chapter 6, we noted how screens promote sedentary behaviour. We'd like to expand on that discussion by exploring the importance of physical activity and being outdoors as two powerful influences on your child's overall health and well-being, providing a buffer against anxiety and stress. Let's begin with looking at the impact of physical activity on the brain.

When people discuss the importance of physical activity for health and well-being, the conversation often focuses on the benefits of that activity on the body or heart. Indeed, most people are acutely aware that exercise is a key factor for staying healthy and fit. It might, however, interest you to know that while many parents earnestly believe that most learning happens in a classroom or at a computer, this learning is actually enhanced by exercise and movement. There is now widespread recognition by health experts, developmental psychologists and neuroscientists alike that not only is physical activity vital for health, good sleep patterns, getting rid of excess energy and socialisation, but it also enhances learning and academic outcomes. In essence, kids who play hard every day may be making their brains, as well as their bodies, stronger. Therefore, as a parent, it is important for you to always bear in mind that physical activity helps your child's brain. Exercise improves emotional regulation, memory and thinking. In fact, research done with children shows that exercise improves verbal ability, mathematical ability, school readiness and self-control. Exercise and physical activity also positively impact on perception and attention, which are both integral to learning and all aspects of development and life.[61] Exercise is so powerful that the brain actually changes when we get moving.

Brain-derived neurotrophic factor (BDNF) sounds very technical, but think of it as "Miracle-Gro" for the brain. When a person exercises, this registers in body and mind as a bit of stress, and BDNF is released into the brain to mediate that stress. In this instance a little bit of stress is helpful, because BDNF changes our neurons and enhances neuroplasticity for the better. It literally is like a fertiliser for the mind. If you couple this exercise with being outdoors, you get more bang for your buck.

Mother Nature is good for us, regardless of our age. One great example is something that was uncovered and published by psychologist Robert Ulrich in 1984. He found that patients who were recovering in hospital rooms with a view of green spaces healed faster, and with less help or intervention, than those in rooms where green spaces could not be looked at.[62] Since that time Ulrich, his collaborators and other researchers have conducted many studies demonstrating the restorative and healing powers of Mother Nature. In relation to the young brains of children, when neuroplasticity is at its peak, exposure to nature has been linked to other benefits, including better attentional control.

Think about this for a moment. Children with ADHD can get the same therapeutic benefits of medication by being outdoors. In 2008, researchers found that children who had been clinically diagnosed with ADHD could concentrate better after a 20-minute walk in the park.[63] In this study, children with ADHD were given a series of puzzles designed to raise attentional fatigue. They were then split into three groups. Each went on a 20-minute "walk-about". One group went through the streets of a downtown concrete jungle, a second meandered through a suburban area clustered with houses, and the third strolled through a vegetation-rich park.

After their walks, the children's attention and executive functioning were tested. Executive functioning refers to several important processes but most notably are those of emotional regulation and higher-order thinking. After the walks, the only group that stood out in terms of their executive functioning was the one that had walked through the park. They performed better on the tests; so much so that the results were as good, or even better, than if they had been medicated with methylphenidate or what is commonly known as Ritalin.

When Shelley was teaching a first-grade class in Sarasota, Florida, some years ago, one boy – let's call him Zack – checked all the boxes for ADHD. In a minute, he could turn a classroom into a zoo. He would lean over and steal a pencil from John, turn and pull Amber's hair, and then rock backwards on his chair and fall over. And yet, once a week, Shelley took the class on a beach walk on Siesta Key and gave Zack the job of leading the class along the intertidal zone and pointing out the various wonders of the rockpools, where his love and interest lay. Perhaps not surprisingly, he demonstrated no ADHD symptoms for the whole two hours. He was fully engaged, responsible, focused and knowledgeable. On returning to the classroom, he was in a calm headspace for the rest of the day and could work and concentrate. This made Shelley consider that perhaps his ADHD symptoms had more to do with the classroom environment than the child's innate "problematic" behaviour.

A more recent study discussing the healing powers of Mother Nature and worth noting was published in 2019. In this study of 900,000 people, researchers found those who had access to a large amount of green space where they lived as children were significantly less likely to be at risk of developing any psychiatric disorders as adults.[64] In other words, being in and around nature as a child meant better mental health as an adult.

These two studies are but a small sample of scientific findings documenting the benefits of being outdoors as much as possible. There is an abundance of evidence showing that childhood exposure to green spaces and the natural environment can be linked to fewer depressive symptoms in adulthood, fewer emotional problems during childhood, and better overall measures of emotional well-being. We also know that when children go outside to play, especially without risk-averse parents hovering around to ensure their child never skins their knees, the benefits go beyond well-being and include such things as building competence and autonomy. All these positives stand in stark contrast with what was discussed earlier: time on screens increasingly shows behavioural and neurological changes associated with both ADHD and autism-like symptoms. So, if you want to help nurture your child's young mind, get them outside hugging and climbing trees rather than looking at them on a screen.

One final note for parents and especially for those of us who are moving on in the circle of life: There is plenty of evidence acknowledging that the ageing brain stays healthier when we exercise. In fact, many processes in the brain stay functional or even improve in older adults who become more physically active. Greater physical activity means a healthier and more vigorous mind, especially as we age. And here is the good news: you don't have to train for a triathlon or follow the mantra of "no pain, no gain"! Thirty minutes of moderate physical activity – essentially going for a brisk walk three to four times a week – is all that is necessary. Couple this with a bit of strength training, resistance for your large muscle groups, and you help your body and mind that much more. At the minimum, however, go for a walk three or four times a week and you will be helping your physical and mental well-being. Make no mistake, exercise not only changes the body but also the mind. This is a great reason to get the whole family together for a jog, a walk, kicking a soccer ball around, or any other form of exercise. Moreover, in prioritising this kind of activity, you are supporting one of the best ways we know to nurture your child's mind. Physical activity, especially outdoors, is more beneficial for you and your child in the long term than worrying about self-esteem, failing or getting a trophy.

Ground Rules

1. Your child is not as fragile as you might think. Allow for risk-taking, challenges and moderately stressful activities. Be sure those activities are age-appropriate but do so knowing that you are building resilience. Put down your shields and roadblocks and allow for mistakes to happen. This will further support resilience and promote the development of a growth mindset.

2. Encourage your child to face challenges with a positive attitude and teach the value of effort and hard work over undeserved praise.

3. Learning from mistakes is a positive endeavour and far healthier than overly focusing on feelings when things go wrong. Get in the habit of asking "What can you do in the future?" rather than "How are your feeling?" when your child is facing adversity. This is a much better approach for your child than being overly concerned about their self-esteem.

4. Teach your child that trophies and awards are something received for excellence above others or oneself as a personal best. Do this with the knowledge that giving everyone a trophy or undeserved gratuitous praise fosters something to be avoided – a fixed mindset.

5. Physical activity and being outdoors nurture the mind as well as the body. This is not only true for your child but also for you. Your parenting will be enhanced if you engage in regular physical activity and take the time to get outdoors.

Ten

Keep Calm and Carry On!

"Caring deeply about our children is part of what makes us human. Yet 'parenting' is a surprisingly new invention. In the past thirty years, the concept of parenting and the huge industry surrounding it have transformed childcare into obsessive, controlling, and goal-oriented labour intended to create a particular kind of child."

– Professor Alison Gopnik[65]

Some Final Thoughts

Keep calm and carry on! Catchy, isn't it? Those five words started to appear on posters in the United Kingdom in 2001. They then went global – or perhaps the oft-used term "viral" is more appropriate. That phrase can now be found on coffee mugs, t-shirts, carry-on luggage and many other objects. But are you aware that it actually emerged almost a century ago?

Sometime in the middle of 1939, "Keep Calm and Carry On" was created by Great Britain's wartime propaganda department, the Ministry of Information. Almost two and a half million posters were printed to help raise the morale of citizens should Britain ever be embroiled in any future wartime activity. This was a time when the memory of World War One was still fresh in people's minds and Adolf Hitler was stretching his power over Europe. Ironically, the vast majority of those posters never saw the light of day. They were pulped and recycled in 1940 to help the British Government overcome a paper shortage as World War Two began to unfold. And it wasn't until the turn of the century that a copy of one of those posters was discovered in a bookstore in Northumberland, with reproductions being sold a year later and its fame established globally.

We like the phrase. We think it is part of the core message of this book. Designed to support a population during any war, "Keep Calm and Carry On" also works across so many other contexts, including parenting. We also think it is a great platform for drawing together all the key messages in this book and a phrase you should keep in the back of your mind when parenting taxes your patience and wants to engage your brain's survival mechanisms. Fight-or-flight is a great short-term solution for life-threatening situations but not so good when your two-year-old decides to make his presence known in a supermarket. With that in mind, let's take a quick look back at some of the key points made in the first nine chapters before we draw some final thoughts together.

At the beginning of this journey, we wanted to offer you a user-friendly guide to understanding the one and a half kilogram universe between our ears. The human brain is certainly one of the universe's most amazing things. Its complexity is still rather poorly understood, but there are some things that we do know.

First, the brain takes a long time to develop and become fully mature; it's not until you are in your mid- to late twenties, depending on whether you are male or female, that you could rightly say you have a mature adult brain. This means that your children see and experience the world through a different lens than you do. It also means that they may act in ways that defy logic, be driven by emotion, and give you reason to question their humanity. Remember, however, that you were once where they are and probably not a perfect child. In fact, there really is no such thing as a "perfect" child, despite what some parents might say. We tend to be creatures with flaws, and the younger we are the more flawed we might appear to be.

Second, the development of the brain's neural connectivity, or architecture, is founded on experience. Experiences matter, and there are things we know that are critical for development and things that shape the brain in a voluntary fashion. At birth, the brain needs to see and hear things for the neural pathways of its visual and auditory systems to develop. Seeing and hearing things early in life are *critical* for the normal and healthy development of those systems. Riding a bike is a bit different.

As children grow and their physical abilities improve, they often extend their independence through new experiences. Getting on a bicycle, balancing, and then eventually riding that bicycle takes time and practice. This is a non-critical experience that will also form neural pathways in the brain. You could effectively call these learning experiences facilitated through interactions with others, whether they be parents, siblings, teachers or friends.

One last neural consideration for parents. Always remember: that 15-year-old – who spends most of their time in the bedroom, grunts or scowls a great deal, often looks half-awake but inhabits an adult-like body – has a brain that is under construction, or more aptly, one that is being renovated. It can be very easy to assume that the teens in your life think like you do. For them, 10 minutes is a lifetime, and they are often turbo-charged with emotion. Their thinking, or the apparent lack thereof, is often driven by a desire for new experiences, new sensations, experimentation and taking risks.

Beyond understanding the changes that are part of your child's normal development, we then offer some insights into how to best support your children as they grow. We look at important avenues in terms of building aspects of resilience to help buffer those challenges that life will often throw our way. Resilience is important for both you and your children and something that can and should be nurtured.

In his seminal work, *The Road Less Travelled*, psychiatrist and author Dr Morgan Scott Peck opens with the following sentiments: "Life is difficult. This is a great truth, one of the greatest truths."[66] Understanding that life is, indeed, difficult at times is important. So too is an understanding that our society, culture and "schooling" are often saturated in a world of 24/7 media which can wreak havoc on resilience and any sense of autonomy. But the world is not a place to be feared. Nor is it a place where you and your children have no sense of agency over how you feel and react and where your only recourse is found within a never-ending industry of self-help or trauma-informed gurus. Every parenting journey is unique – a "road less travelled". In fact, each child takes their parents on a journey where certainly parts of the road have never been travelled. And most children require, at some point, that parents go off-road – following their wisdom, their insights, their understanding of their children. This book is not a roadmap, rather an encouraging guide and reminder that you matter, your wisdom matters and your presence in your children's lives is the most important element in their environment. You are the best medicine for you and your children. You know yourself and your children well. This is something that you must always remember when the best intentions of others may not be very helpful at all. Perhaps a recent example will help to demonstrate our concerns.

In Chapter 5 we explored issues around how schools and educators, with all good intentions, are not always the best avenues for supporting mental health via any measure of "trauma-informed" practice. This has become increasingly important given the rise of mental health issues in children and particularly in teens as reported by many government departments and health practitioners. And while we might think that any outside support, be it from schools or elsewhere, is beneficial, a recent study suggests otherwise.

Researchers from the School of Psychology at the University of Sydney examined the outcomes of an eight-week school-based behavioural intervention to determine what its impact was on the mental health of its 1071 student participants.[67] These students were roughly 14 years old, and what the researchers found was very interesting. It turns out that those who received the school-based intervention actually demonstrated significantly poorer outcomes than when they began the program! That's right, you read it correctly. The intervention not only did not help – it made things worse. The question is why?

First, let's start with the realisation that an important part of the transition into becoming an adult is identity formation. Adolescents are in the process of finding out, and shaping, who they are. Pop culture, particularly movies, provides familiar examples. From Danny Zuko (John Travolta) in *Grease*, who struggles between being the leader of the T-Birds and becoming a clean-cut athlete to impress Sandy Olsson (Olivia Newton-John), to the vampires and werewolves in *Twilight*, identify formation is a central theme in those and many other films. Identity formation in teens, however, is far more important than just being a catalyst for a well-written screenplay. Teens are especially prone to take labels, especially psychological labels, to heart.

Second, given that identity formation is so important, could it be that continually ruminating about mental health issues might actually be exacerbating any problems? The study noted above seems to suggest as much and may be further evidence of what has become known as "prevalence inflation".[68] Prevalence inflation suggests that greater awareness of mental illness leads people to talk about normal life struggles in terms of "symptoms" and "diagnoses". In previous generations, a teen might have said "I am nervous about something" but now is more likely to say "I can't do something because I have anxiety". Interventions and the diffusion of online psychological self-help diagnoses and therapeutic language have encouraged people to view the everyday challenges of life as insurmountable or something to be diagnosed and treated. Labels such as "symptoms" and "diagnoses" dictate how people view themselves in ways that can become self-fulfilling and shape their identity. Simply stated, the more you focus on how you feel and the idea that those feelings need to be "fixed", the more likely you are to make those feelings worse and diminish any forms of resilience.

That is some of the bad news, but here is the good news and where you come in. One of the other findings of the study done by the researchers from the University of Sydney was that some students engaged in behavioural interventions at home rather than school and with the help of parents did much better. Now don't misunderstand us here, as we are not suggesting that you suddenly engage in prescribed therapeutic practices. Instead, we think it important to emphasise the fundamental message that parents play the most important role in the mental health of their children and need not rely on schools to do so. You can act to ensure that your and your children's mental health, sense of self and spirits are kept intact. And at the risk of being repetitive, this is about building resilience and fostering a sense of hope and optimism.

Building resilience is part and parcel of being self-aware. That is why we provided, throughout many of the chapters, food for thought in terms of how you, as part of your parenting repertoire, can take care of yourself. In a sense, that is perhaps the foundation of this book. Knowing who *you* are and taking steps to ensure you stay grounded is central to ensuring you can offer the best environment for your children. Being grounded also means you exude optimism and hope in a world hell-bent on making people aware of any and every "crisis".

Fear, born out of news of one crisis after another, was part of the discussion related to anxiety and stress in Chapter 7. It seems that every time we turn on the news there is a looming crisis at our doorstep. We mentioned "global boiling" as a current crisis. In our own lifetimes we have seen many crises come and go: the population explosion narrative of the 1960s and 1970s, acid rain, holes in the ozone layer, global warming, global cooling, climate change and Y2K to name a few. Yet we have survived, despite the doomsayers and Nostradamus wannabes. And while there are certainly problems around the globe, humanity and human societies are generally doing much better than previous generations.

In 2018, acclaimed author and Harvard psychologist Professor Steven Pinker's book *Enlightenment Now* hit the shelves of bookstores around the world. In it, he argues that life has been getting better for the vast majority of humankind. He documents 15 different measures of human well-being, along with the evidence and stats, to support his position. He notes that people live longer and healthier lives on average than ever before and that any "bleak assessment of the state of the world is wrong. And not just a little wrong – wrong wrong, flat-earth wrong, couldn't be more wrong".[69]

The position set out by Professor Pinker is difficult to dispute given the evidence he presents. We think his work should be required reading in all high schools. This might counter-balance the narratives presented across most media and social media platforms. Consider also that the word "crisis" is derived from the ancient Greek verb "krinein" meaning to judge in order to make a decision. Perhaps it is time to make more optimistic judgements and decisions by being grounded with a sense of hope and optimism for the future. We believe that being this far into the 21st century has provided more than enough evidence that things are okay. Sure, there will always be challenges, but ruminating over them only leads to anxiety and stress. Instead, carve a path forward for you and your children to enjoy the world around you, and when things do go awry, remember that you are the buffer between your children and that very world. What type of buffer do you want to be?

That's where Chapters 8 and 9 come in. One asks you to take care of yourself! You won't be any good to your children if you are anxious or stressed or in a state of chaos. The second provides some thoughts on how to extend your care into that of your children. We are realists, however, and recognise that children and teens, at times, are chaotic, messy, unpredictable and tiresome. They are also joyful, energetic and humorous and can brighten any day. Because of this, your parenting journey, by its very nature, will be off-road. If there was one single manual for being a parent, we all would have it and it would be practised across generations. In lieu of such a manual, the following words offer a foundation for what we believe and have written in this book:

> The purpose of loving children, in particular, is to give those helpless young human beings a rich, stable, safe environment – an environment in which variation, innovation, and novelty can blossom… Loving children doesn't give them a destination; it gives them sustenance for the journey.[70]

Providing sustenance for the journey means you need to be at your best as much as possible. It recognises that the millions of possible variations that might impact on the life of a family, its individuals and their relationships means the path of raising a child into adulthood will be rough – and the best you can do is take care of yourself and stay grounded.

The Golden Ground Rule

Take care of yourself, don't sweat the small stuff, and keep calm and carry on!

About the Authors

Michael Nagel is an educator, researcher, author and most importantly a parent. He is the author of twenty-one books focusing broadly on educational psychology, child and adolescent development and parenting. Michael is a prolific speaker and aside from his teaching and research activity as an Associate Professor at The University of the Sunshine Coast, he has presented to more than 400 audiences across many countries. He has been a feature writer for the 'The First Five Years' online parenting platform and for 'Jigsaw' and the 'Child' series of magazines which collectively offers parenting advice to more than one million parents. As he mellows with age he finds his greatest joys in life are sharing it with his partner, Laura, and being a father to two amazing people finding their way in the world, Madeline and Harrison.

Shelley Davidow is an award-winning international author who grew up in South Africa. Writing across genres, her 50 books reflect her experiences living and working on five continents over two decades. Recent publications include the memoirs *Runaways* (Ultimo, 2022), *Shadow Sisters* (University of Queensland Press, 2018), *Whisperings in the Blood* (University of Queensland Press, 2016), and the parenting book, *Raising Stressproof Kids* (Exisle Publishing, 2014). Her day job is as a senior lecturer in Education at the University of the Sunshine Coast in Queensland. She's also a facilitator in Restorative Practice and consults with schools and communities around the country. In the time that's left over, she runs creative writing workshops, and is also a HeartMath coach and mentor. She lives near a saltwater lake with her family and some tame kookaburras.

Endnotes

1. Eagleman (2020), p. 3.
2. Abbott (2013), p. 274. Bill Bryson captures this and other amazing facts about the brain in his 2019 book entitled *The Body*.
3. Hart & Risley (1995).
4. Theory of mind is the ability to understand another person's thoughts and perspective. Research noted includes Bialystok & Martin (2004), Craik et al (2010), and Kovács (2009).
5. See Miendlarzewska & Trost (2014) and Stoklosa (2016).
6. Sapolsky (2004), p. 98.
7. McCraty (2003); McCraty & Childre (2002).
8. McCraty et al. (2001).
9. McCraty et al. (2001).
10. Pribram & Rozman (1997).
11. McCraty et al. (2001), p. 7.
12. McCraty et al. (2001), p. 18.
13. McCraty et al. (2009), p. 61.
14. Walsh (2004), pp. 187–88.
15. Hall (1904).
16. The work of Dr Jean M. Twenge, Professor of Psychology at San Diego State University, is replete with evidence related to the decline of adolescent mental health; in particular her book entitled *iGen: Why Today's Super-Connected Kids are Growing Up Less Rebellious, More Tolerant, Less Happy and Completely Unprepared for Adulthood* is worth a read.
17. See Nagel (2021a), Nagel (2021b) and Sharman & Nagel (2022) for some preliminary insights into issues related to screen devices and development.
18. This pilot study was conducted in Australia but could not be finalised because restrictions resulting from the pandemic negated any opportunity to gather more data and publish the findings.
19. Cozolino (2013), p. 215.
20. McCraty et al. (2022).
21. Felitti et al. (1998).
22. See Shonkoff (2010). The original taxonomy for this work was published in 2005 by the United States National Council on the Developing Child.
23. Callaway (2013).

24 Bruce McEwan, mentioned in the previous paragraph, wrote extensively on the mind's ability to create a physiological response to stress, even in the absence of stressful or threatening factors. See McEwan & Lasley (2002), for example.
25 Sommers & Satel (2005).
26 A good starting point would be Gray (2019).
27 The content on schools in Finland is derived from the work of Professor Pasi Sahlberg (2010). Professor Sahlberg was the primary architect for restructuring education in Finland and currently is a staff member at both the University of Melbourne and the Gonski Institute for Education in Australia.
28 OECD (2021).
29 Twenge (2017), p. 299.
30 Schleicher's comments can be found in the introduction of the OECD (2015) report.
31 A good starting point source for looking at the impact of violent video games is Warburton & Braunstein (2012).
32 Ginott (2023).
33 Harvard researchers published these findings about two decades ago. See Lockley et al. (2003).
34 For an interesting and reader-friendly look at how dopamine drives us, see Dr Anna Lembke's book *Dopamine Nation*.
35 Olivia Solon broke the news regarding Sean Parker in 2017.
36 See Barthorpe et al. (2020).
37 Centres for Disease Control and Prevention (2021).
38 Zamfir (2018).
39 If you are interested in looking at some of the studies noted, see Gwynette et al. (2018); Slobodin et al. (2019); Chen et al. (2020); Heffler et al. (2020, 2022); Hutton et al. (2020); Dong et al. (2021) and Kushima et al. (2022).
40 Gardner (2009), pp. 6 and 10.
41 Sun & Eisenman (2021).
42 Dweck (2017).
43 Hansberry et al. (2014).
44 Rickard & White (2021).
45 Childre & Paddison (1996).
46 Grille (2005); Nagel (2012a).
47 McCraty (2015), p. 36.
48 McCraty (2015), p. 41.
49 McCraty (2015), p. 27.
50 Song et al. (2023).
51 Pressman et al. (2013).
52 Do an online search for any of these for descriptions and rules.
53 Nagel (2012b), p. 190.
54 See Gardner (2009); Hupp & Jewell (2015); Lukianoff & Haidt (2018); Pinker (2018).

55 Davidow & Williams (2017).
56 Dweck (2017).
57 The work related to addiction and escaping from pain by Dr Anna Lembke (2021) makes for compelling reading in this area.
58 Baumeister et al. (2003) present a robust review of the research around self-esteem and performance.
59 Lukianhoff & Haidt (2018). See also Almas et al. (2010); Kanngiesser & Warneken (2012); Sloane et al. (2012).
60 *The Narcissism Epidemic* by Jean Twenge and W. Keith Campbell (2009) is meticulous in detail, supported by a large body of evidence, and provides extensive details on this topic.
61 Michael's book *In the Beginning* (2012a), which focused on brain development in children, has detailed information and research on the impact of physical activity on a child's developing brain. It is also significant to note that while exercise is important for all children, it is a biological imperative for boys (see Nagel, 2021).
62 Ulrich (1984).
63 Taylor & Kuo (2008).
64 Engemann et al. (2019).
65 This eloquent quote is from the back cover of Professor Gopnik's 2016 book entitled *The Gardener and The Carpenter*.
66 Peck (1978).
67 Harvey et al. (2023).
68 Foulkes & Andrews (2023).
69 Pinker (2018), p. xv.
70 Gopnik (2016), p.10.

References

Abbott, A. (2013). Solving the brain. *Nature, 499*(7458), 272.
Almås, I., Cappelan, A. W., Sørenson, E. Ø., & Tungodden, B. (2010). Fairness and the development of inequality acceptance. *Science, 328,* 1176-78.
Barthorpe, A., Winstone, L., Mars, B., & Moran, P. (2020). Is social media screen time really associated with poor adolescent mental health? A time use diary study. *Journal of Affective Disorders, 274,* 864-70.
Baumeister, R. F., Campbell, J. D., Krueger, J. I., & Voh, K. D. (2003). Does high self-esteem cause better performance, interpersonal success, happiness, or healthier lifestyles? *Psychological Science in the Public Interest, 4*(1), 1-44.
Bialystok, E., & Martin, M. M. (2004). Attention and inhibition in bilingual children: Evidence from the dimensional change card sorting task. *Developmental Science, 7*(3), 325-39.
Bryson, B. (2019). *The body: A guide for occupants.* Doubleday.
Callaway, E. (2013). Fearful memories haunt mouse descendants. *Nature, 1,* 1-6.
Centres for Disease Control and Prevention (CDC) (2021). *Morbidity and Mortality Weekly Report Surveillance Summaries, 70*(11).
Chen, J. Y., Strodl, E., Wu, C. A., Huang, L. H., Yin, X. N., & Wen, G. M. (2020). Screen time and autistic-like behaviors among preschool children in China. Psychology, *Health & Medicine, 5,* 607-620.
Childre, D. L., & Paddison, S. H. (1996). *Teaching children to love: 80 games & fun activities for raising balanced children in unbalanced times.* Planetary Publications.
Cozolino, L. (2013). *The social neuroscience of education: Optimizing attachment and learning in the classroom.* W. W. Norton & Company.
Craik, F. I. M., Bialystok, E., & Freedman, M. (2010). Delaying the onset of Alzheimer disease: Bilingualism as a form of cognitive reserve. *Neurology, 75*(19), 1726-29.
Davidow, S., & Williams, P. (2017). F*ail brilliantly: Exploding the myths of failure and success.* Familius.
Dias, B.G., & Ressler, K. J. (2014). Parental olfactory experience influences behavior and neural structure in subsequent generations. *Nature Neuroscience, 17*(1), 89-96.
Dong, H. Y., Wang, B., Li, H. H., Yue, X. J., & Jia, F. Y. (2021). Correlation between screen time and autistic symptoms as well as development quotients in children with autistic spectrum disorder. *Frontiers in Psychiatry, 12,* 619994.

Dweck, C. S. (2017). *Mindset: Changing the way you think to fulfil your potential* (7th ed.). Little, Brown Book Group.

Eagleman, D. (2020). *Livewired: The inside story of the ever-changing brain.* Pantheon Books.

Engemann, K., Pedersen, C. B., Arge, L., Tsirogiannis, C., Mortensen, P. B., & Svenning, J. C. (2019). Residential green space in childhood is associated with lower risk of psychiatric disorders from adolescence into adulthood. *Proceedings of the National Academy of Sciences, 116*(11), 5188-193.

Felitti, V. J., Anda, R. F., Nordenberg, D., Williamson, D. F., Spitz, A. M., Edwards, V., Koss, M. P., & Marks, J. S. (1998). Relationship of childhood abuse and household dysfunction to many of the leading causes of death in adults: The Adverse Childhood Experiences (ACE) study. *American Journal of Preventative Medicine, 14*(4), 245-58.

Foulkes, L., & Andrews, J. L. (2023). Are mental health awareness efforts contributing to the rise in reported mental health problems? A call to test the prevalence inflation hypothesis. *New Ideas in Psychology, 69*:101010.

Gardner, D. (2009). *The science of fear: How the culture of fear manipulates your brain.* Plume.

Ginott, H. (2023) Quotes.net. Retrieved 13 September 2023 from https://www.quotes.net/quote/40429.

Goldstein, R., & Volkow, N. (2011). Dysfunction of the prefrontal cortex in addiction: Neuroimaging findings and clinical implications. *Nature Reviews Neuroscience, 12*, 652-69.

Gopnik, A. (2016). *The gardener and the carpenter: What the new science of child development tells us about the relationship between parents and children.* Vintage.

Gray, P. (2019). Evolutionary functions of play: Practice, resilience, innovation, and cooperation. In P. K. Smith & J. L. Roopnarine (Eds.), *The Cambridge handbook of play: Developmental and disciplinary perspectives* (pp. 84-102). Cambridge University Press.

Grille, R. (2005). *Parenting for a peaceful world.* Longueville Media.

Gwynette, M. F., Sidhu, S. S., & Ceranoglu, T. A. (2018). Electronic screen media use in youth with autism spectrum disorder. *Child and Adolescent Psychiatric Clinics of North America, 27*(2), 203-219.

Hall, G. S. (1904). *Adolescence: Its psychology and its relations to physiology, anthropology, sociology, sex, crime, religion, and education.* Appleton Press.

Hansberry, W., Williams, S., Lennox, J. B., George, G., Abramson, L., Hutchison, K., & Casey, M. (2014). *The psychology of emotion in restorative practice: How affect script psychology explains how and why restorative practice works.* Jessica Kingsley Publishers.

Hart, B., & Risley, T. R. (1995). *Meaningful differences in the everyday experience of young American children.* Brookes Publishing.

Harvey, L. J., White, F. A., Hunt, C., & Abbott, M. (2023). Investigating the efficacy of a dialectical behaviour therapy-based universal intervention on adolescent social and emotional well-being outcomes. *Behaviour Research and Therapy, 169*: 104408.

Heffler, K. F., Frome, L. R., & Gullo, D. F. (2022). Changes in autism symptoms associated with screen exposure: Case report of two young children. *Psychiatry Research Case Studies, 1*(2).

Heffler, K. F., Sienko, D. M., Subedi, K., McCann, K. A., & Bennett, D. S. (2020). Association of early-life social and digital media experiences with development of autism spectrum disorder-like symptoms. *JAMA Pediatrics, 174*(7) 690–96.

Hupp, S., & Jewell, J. (2015). *Great myths of child development.* Wiley Blackwell.

Hutton, J. S., Dudley, J., Horowitz-Kraus, T., DeWitt, T., & Holland, S. K. (2020). Associations between screen-based media use and brain white matter integrity in preschool-aged children. *JAMA Pediatrics, 174*(1), e193869.

Ikhlaq, A., Buzdar, A. S, et. al., (2023). Phasic Induction of bioelectromagnetic heart-brain coupling through emotional stimuli. *Journal of Xi'an Shiyou University, Natural Science Edition, 19*(4), 271–94.

Kanngiesser, P., & Warneken, F. (2012). Young children consider merit when sharing resources with others. *PLOS ONE, 7*(8), e43979.

Koepp, M. J., Gunn, R. N., Lawrence, A. D., Cunningham, V. J., Dagher, A., Jones, T., Brooks, D. J., Bench, C. J., & Grasby, P. M. (1998). Evidence for striatal dopamine release during a video game. *Nature, 393*(6682), 266–68.

Kovács Á. M. (2009). Early bilingualism enhances mechanisms of false-belief reasoning. *Developmental Science 12*(1), 48–54.

Kushima, M., Kojima, R., Shinohara, R., Horiuchi, S., Otawa, S., Ooka, T., Akiyama, Y., Miyake, K., Yokomichi, H., & Yamagata, Z. (2022); Japan Environment and Children's Study Group. Association between screen time exposure in children at 1 year of age and autism spectrum disorder at 3 years of age: The Japan Environment and Children's Study. *JAMA Pediatrics, 176*(4), 384–91.

Lembke, A. (2021). *Dopamine nation: Finding balance in the age of indulgence.* Headline Publishing Group.

Lockley, S. W., Brainard, G. C., & Czeisler, C. A. (2003). High sensitivity of the human circadian melatonin rhythm to resetting short wavelength light. *The Journal of Clinical Endocrinology & Metabolism, 88*(9), 4502–5.

Lukianoff, G. & Haidt, J. (2018). *The coddling of the American mind: How good intentions and bad ideas are setting up a generation for failure.* Penguin Press.

McCraty, R. (2003). *The heart as a hormonal gland.* Institute of HeartMath. http://www.heartmath.org/research/science-of-the-heart/soh_6.html.

McCraty, R. (2015). Energetic communication. In *Science of the heart: An overview of research conducted by the HeartMath Institute.* Vol. 2. HeartMath Institute.https://www.heartmath.org/research/science-of-the-heart/energetic-communication/

McCraty, R. (2022). Following the rhythm of the heart: HeartMath Institute's path to HRV biofeedback. *Applied Psychophysiology and Biofeedback, 47*(4), 305–316.

McCraty, R., & Childre, D. (2002). *The appreciative heart: The psychophysiology of positive emotions and optimal functioning.* Institute of HeartMath.

McEwan, B., & Lasley, E. N. (2002). *The end of stress as we know it.* Joseph Henry Press.

Miendlarzewska, E. A., & Trost, W. J. (2014). How musical training affects cognitive development: Rhythm, reward and other modulating variables. *Frontiers in Neuroscience, 7*(279), 1-18.

Nagel, M. C. (2012a). *In the beginning: The brain, early development and learning.* Australian Council for Educational Research.

Nagel, M. C. (2012b). *Nurturing a healthy mind: Doing what matters most for your child's developing brain.* Exisle Publishing.

Nagel, M. C. (2021a). *Oh boy! Understanding the neuroscience behind educating and raising boys.* Amba Press.

Nagel, M. C. (2021b). *It's a girl thing! Understanding the neuroscience behind educating and raising girls.* Amba Press.

Nagel. M. C. (2012). *In the beginning: The brain, early development and learning.* Australian Council for Educational Research (ACER).

National Scientific Council on the Developing Child (2005). *Excessive stress disrupts the architecture of the developing brain* (Working Paper No. 3). Available at: https://developingchild.harvard.edu/resources/wp3

OECD (2015). *Students, computers and learning: Making the connection.* OECD Publishing.

OECD (2021). *Supporting young people's mental health through the COVID-19 crisis. OECD Policy Responses to Coronavirus (COVID-19).* OECD Publishing.

Peck, M.S. (1978). *The road less travelled: A new psychology of love, traditional values and spiritual growth.* Touchstone – Simon & Schuster.

Pinker, S. (2018). *Enlightenment now: The case for reason, science, humanism and progress.* Allen Lane.

Pressman, S. D., Gallagher, M. W., & Lopez, S. J. (2013) Is the emotion-health connection a "first-world problem?" *Psychological Science, 24*(4), pp. 544-49.

Pribram, K., & Rozman, D. (1997). Early childhood development and learning: What new research on the heart and brain tells us about our youngest children. In *White House Satellite Conference on Early Childhood Development and Learning*, San Francisco.

Rickard, S. C., & White, M. P. (2021). Barefoot walking, nature connectedness and psychological restoration: The importance of stimulating the sense of touch for feeling closer to the natural world. *Landscape Research, 46*(7), 975-91.

Sahlberg, P. (2010). *Finnish lessons: What can the world learn from educational change in Finland?* Teachers College Press.

Sapolsky, R. (2004). *Why zebras don't get ulcers.* Owl Books.

Sharman, R., & Nagel, M. C. (2022). *Becoming autistic: How technology is altering the minds of the next generation.* Amba Press.

Shonkoff, J. P. (2010). Building a new biodevelopmental framework to guide the future of early childhood policy. *Child Development, 81*(1), 357-67.

Sloane, S., Baillargeon, R., & Premack, D. (2012). Do infants have a sense of fairness? *Psychological Science, 23*(2), 196-204.

Slobodin, O., Heffler, K. F., & Davidovitch, M. (2019). Screen media and autism spectrum disorder: A systematic literature review. *Journal of Developmental Behavioral Pediatrics, 40*(4), 303-311.

Solon, O. (2017). Ex-Facebook president Sean Parker: Site made to exploit human vulnerability. *Guardian*, 9 November 2017.

Sommers, C. H., & Satel, S. (2005). *One nation under therapy: How the helping culture is eroding self-reliance.* St Martin's Griffin.

Song, C. F., Tay, P. K. C., Gwee, X., Wee, S. L., & Ng, T. P. (2023). Happy people live longer because they are healthy people. *BMC Geriatrics, 23*(1), 440.

Stoklosa, A. R. (2016). Instruments of knowledge: Music and the brain. *The Review: A Journal of Undergraduate Student Research, 17*(1), 12.

Sun, S., & Eisenman, I. (2021), Observed Antarctic sea ice expansion reproduced in a climate model after correcting biases in sea ice drift velocity. *Nature Communications, 12*(1), 1-6.

Taylor, A. F., & Kuo, F. E. (2008). Children with attention deficits concentrate better after walk in the park. *Journal of Attention Disorders, 12*(5), 402-9.

Twenge, J. M., & Campbell, W. K. (2009). *The narcissism epidemic: Living in the age of entitlement.* Atria.

Twenge, J. M. (2017). *iGen: Why today's super-connected kids are growing up less rebellious, more tolerant, less happy and completely unprepared for adulthood.* Atria Books.

Ulrich, R. S. (1984). View through a window may influence recovery from surgery. *Science, 224*(4647), 420-21.

Walsh, D. (2004). *Why do they act that way? A survival guide to the adolescent brain for you and your teen.* Free Press.

Warburton, W., & Braunstein, D. (Eds.) (2012). *Growing up fast and furious: Reviewing the impacts of violent and sexualised media on children.* Federation Press.

Zamfir, M. T. (2018). The consumption of virtual environment for more than 4 hours/day, in children between 0-3 years old, can cause a syndrome similar with the autism spectrum disorder. *Journal of Romanian Literary Studies, 13*, 953-68.

Index

abuse 54-55
accountability 99-100
activism 72-75, 78, 95
addiction 46, 88-89
adolescence 39-51, 148-149
adrenaline 32, 49
adulthood 19, 29, 51
adverse childhood experiences 54-57
adversity 26, 57, 131-132, 143
aggression 84-85
alcohol 43-44
amygdala 26, 43-44
anxiety 5, 10, 16, 26, 44, 50, 60-65, 71-72, 130-143, 149-150
Apple iPhone 47
appreciation 36, 117
apps 84-90
arts 7
attachment 35
attention 43, 50
attention deficit hyperactivity disorder (ADHD) 90, 140-142
autism spectrum disorders (ASD) 90-93

Bandura, Albert 63
barefoot 106
behaviour 39-42, 46-47, 58, 62-63, 77-78, 150
big tech 85, 89
bilingual 15, 18-19, 23
biofeedback technique 53
birth 12-13
blue light 87-88
boys 69-70
brain 9-22, 30-37, 40
brain development 5, 9. 12, 15, 22, 59, 146-147
brain science 17
brain-derived neurotrophic factor (BDNF) 139-140
breathing 53-54, 61

calm 63-64, 118, 145-152
care 7, 111-127
cherry blossoms 58
childhood 1, 54-55
Chilton-Pearce, Joseph 111
climate issues 73-74, 95-97, 150-151
cognitive development 5, 19
cognitive function 29, 37, 47
coherence 33, 36
coherent 116-119, 123
compassion 7, 77
computers 45, 81-84
concentration 19, 43
conception 10-11
conflict 57-58, 102-103
connection 11-13, 105-110, 122-123
consistency 22
Cooper, Sheldon 90
cortisol 26, 49, 107, 114, 118
Cozolino, Louis 53
crawling 59

death 29, 54
decision-making 41-42, 45
dementia 19
depression 50, 57, 87-88
deprivation 17
deviance 70
diabetes 57
diagnoses 91, 149
diet 61
digital detox 50, 92-93
dinner time 105
displacement hypothesis 46-47
diversity 7, 74
divorce 56
doom 74, 81, 150-151
dopamine 42, 49, 88-89, 107-108
drugs 43, 88-89
Dweck, Carol 98, 134-135

165

early development 9
early years learning 68–71
educational practices 6
effort 43, 98, 108, 135–138
electrocardiogram 116
electromagnetic field 33, 115
emotional skills 47
emotions 21, 33–34, 51
enrichment 16–19
environment 28, 37, 42, 45, 96–97
epigenetics 11, 58, 61
epinephrine 32
ethics 48
eustress 56, 64
executive functioning 141–142
exercise 61–62, 86–87, 139–143
experience-dependent growth 46
experience-expectant stimulation 18
experiences 13, 44–45, 54–55, 80–81, 85, 147

Facebook 89
failure 132–135
fear 28–31, 37, 58, 134–135
fear 95–98, 104, 148
fight-or-fight 25–28, 32, 37, 53, 62–63, 97, 109, 113, 120, 146
Finland 71–72
fixed mindset 134–135
food 43, 61, 123
fragile 136–138
frontal lobes 20–21, 42–43
frustration 36, 117

games 123–127
Gardner, Daniel 95
Gen Z 80
genes 58
Giedd, Jay 46
Ginott, Haim 85
global boiling 96
global panic 3
goals 98–99
Google 89
Gopnick, Alison 145
government 6, 60, 82–83
gratitude 33–34, 36, 97, 114, 123
green space 141–142
grey matter 15–16
grounded 2, 7, 36, 108
growth mindset 7, 98–103, 134–135, 143

Hall, Stanley G. 40
happiness 47, 123, 126
happy 35, 123, 126–127
harm 48, 90, 99–100
Harris, Tristan 89
healthy adults 2, 28
healthy development 5, 47–48, 51, 129–131, 147
heart 5, 7, 27–29, 33–37, 53, 56
heart disease 29, 57
heart rate 27, 29–30, 34–37, 62
heart rate variability 34–35, 117
HeartMath 29–30, 33–37, 54, 113–118, 123
heart-to-brain messages 34
helicopter parents 131–132
high coherence 36–37
high variability 34–35
higher-order thinking 21
Hoff Sommers, Christina 67
home environment 5, 7
homework 71–72
hope 150–151
hormones 30, 39
humour 125–127

identity 44, 149
ideological pathways 3
independence 44–45, 51, 147
injury 57–58
instrument 19, 23
intelligence 17, 19, 33
intensive early screen exposure (IESE) 91–92
interactions 42, 47, 75, 91, 147
internet 45, 80–83, 107

joy 123–127
judgement 41, 135, 151
justice 100, 137–138

kindergarten 68–71

language development 14, 18
learning environment 7, 71–72
learning window 18–19
LeDoux, Joseph 10
life satisfaction 47
limbic system 21–22
literacy development 13, 59
lobes 20–21
lockdowns 75–76

love 33, 36, 103–110
low variability 35
Luddites 51, 80

maternal stress 11
maturation 20–21, 40–42
McCraty, Rollin 34, 37
McEwan, Bruce 61
media 6, 60, 62, 75, 151
meditation 61, 114
melatonin 87–88
meltdown 118–119
memory 43, 58
mental health 40, 46–50, 61, 75–78, 149–150
mind 5, 7, 130–143
mindfulness 61–62
mindsets 98–103, 134–135
moods 43–44
Mother Nature 9, 12, 92–93, 139–143
motivation 43, 137
motor coordination 16
movement 43, 69–70
Mozart 17
MTV 46
musical instrument 19, 23, 98
myelin 15–16, 41
mythinformation 18

National Assessment Program - Literacy and Numeracy (NAPLAN) 71–72
NASA 133
nature 2, 7, 13, 45, 82, 106–107, 141–142
neglect 57
nervous system 30, 34, 53–54, 96–97, 114–115
neural development 18
neurobiological processes 33–34
neurons 10–11, 15–16, 41, 140
neuroscience 10, 16, 33
neurotransmitters 43
news 6, 62, 95–97, 132
normal development 13, 147
nurture 13, 45, 60

offroad 2, 108, 148
optimism 150–151
oral language 13–14, 69–70
Organisation for Economic and Co-operative Development (OECD) 82
outdoors 141–143

overachievers 28
oxytocin 33

pandemic 3, 49, 87
panic attacks 53–54
parasympathetic nervous system 30, 35, 96
parental responsibilities 4
parentese 14
Parker, Sean 89
peers 50–51, 72, 75, 82, 137
perfect child 2, 146–147
physical development 19
physical health 61, 86–87, 92, 139–143
physiology 40, 123, 126
Pinker, Steve 151
play 2, 7, 13–15, 23, 69, 107, 139
play-based learning 69–72
positive environment 37, 126
positive stress 56–57, 64
positivity 6, 51, 64–65, 123, 143
post-traumatic stress disorder 3, 58
praise 98–99, 135–139
prefrontal lobes 41
pregnancy 11–12, 22, 26
preschool 68–71
prevalence inflation 149
Programme for International Student Assessment (PISA) 83
pruning 41–42
pubescence 39–40
punishment 10–103

quick coherence technique 54, 113–121, 127

relationships 7, 22, 29–30, 56, 70. 103
repetition 12, 22
resilience 6, 53–65, 79–93, 131–143, 147
responsibility 99–100
restorative practices 99–103, 118–120
rewards 43, 51, 62, 88–89, 138
risk-taking 41–42, 44, 50–51, 143
role model 51, 92
routines 22, 75–76

safe spaces 2, 55, 80
safety 53–55
Sapolsky, Robert 26
Satel, Sally 67
school readiness 14, 69–71, 140
schooling 6–7, 48, 50, 60, 69, 76, 148

schools 3-4, 54-55, 59-60, 64, 67-78, 136-137, 148-149
Scott Peck, Morgan 148
screen devices 15-17, 45-49, 79-83, 139-143
screen time 48-49, 51, 83-86, 104-110
second language 18-19, 23
sedentary behaviour 86-87
self-acceptance 67
self-care 122-124, 127
self-discovery 53
self-esteem 47, 136-138
self-worth 134-135
sensation-seeking 43, 50-51
sex 43, 88-89
sharing 137-138
Shonkoff, John 56
siblings 99-103
sight 12, 18
Silicon Valley 89
sleep 43, 50, 61, 87-88, 112
smartphones 45-51, 81-82, 86-93
smell 10, 12-13, 58
snowplough parents 131-132
social activity 50
social justice 73-74
social learning theory 63
social media 6, 51, 75, 104-110, 151
social skills 13, 47
socio-emotional development 5
speech 14, 22
stimulation 19
storm 29, 40-41, 121
stress 2, 5, 10, 16, 22, 25-37, 40, 44, 54-57, 60-65, 71-72
stress freeway 2, 32
stress hormones 30-32
stress response 27-28, 30-31, 49, 58, 76, 114
stress tolerance 63-64
stress-proof 33
substance abuse 55-57
success 112-113
survival 21, 44, 96-97
sympathetic nervous system 30, 34, 96, 115
symptoms 91, 141-142, 149
synapses 10-12, 41-43

talking 14-15
taste 12-13
teachable moments 63, 135
teachers 29, 55-56, 67-68, 71-78
technology 6, 28, 45-47, 79-93
teens 5, 40-41, 79-80, 149
testing 71-72, 82-83
theory of mind 19
therapy 60, 67, 73-75, 149
thinking 4, 21, 32, 42-43, 85, 114, 122, 133, 139
tiredness 50
tolerable stress 56-57, 64
toxic stress 57, 64
transition 39-40, 149
trauma 3, 5-6, 53-65, 75-78, 148-149
triggers 62
tweens 5, 40
Twenge, Jean M. 79
twins 130

Ulrich, Robert 140
utero 5, 10, 22, 27

verbal language 14, 22
video games 84-85, 89
violence 55-58, 76-77, 84-85
virtual autism 91-92
virtual reality 49
virtual worlds 46, 85-86, 131
visual stimulation 13, 16
vocabulary 14

Walsh, David 39
well-being 47, 64, 71, 83, 122, 139, 142
Williams, Paul 133
wisdom 53, 148
world fears 6
world view 3-4
World War Two 145-146

yoga 61, 114

Zamfir, Marius 91-92
Zen 32
Zuckerberg, Mark 89

www.ingramcontent.com/pod-product-compliance
Lightning Source LLC
Chambersburg PA
CBHW052133110526
44591CB00012B/1710